selling
houses

How to sell your house as quickly as you can
for as much money as you can

Anthea Masey
with Andrew Winter

headline

Text Copyright © Anthea Masey 2003
Foreword and tips © Andrew Winter 2003

The right of Anthea Masey to be identified as the Author
of the Work has been asserted by her in accordance
with the Copyright, Designs and Patents Act 1988.

First published in 2003
by HEADLINE BOOK PUBLISHING

First published in paperback in 2004
by HEADLINE BOOK PUBLISHING

10 9 8 7 6 5 4 3 2

Cataloguing in Publication Data is available from the British Library

Special photography by Paul Bricknell
Full picture credits are given on page 160.

Designed by Dan Newman at Perfect Bound Ltd

Printed and Bound in Great Britain by Butler and Tanner Ltd, Frome, Somerset
Colour Reproduction by Radstock Repro

The prices given for properties were accurate at the time
the programmes were made.

The author, their assigns, licensees and printers cannot accept any liability for any
errors or omissions contained herein nor liability for any loss to any person acting
as a result of the information contained in the book. This book gives advice on
the basis that readers contemplating selling their homes takes their own
professional advice.

ISBN 0 7553 1233 3

HEADLINE BOOK PUBLISHING
A division of Hodder Headline
338 Euston Road
London NW1 3BH

www.headline.co.uk

contents

introduction

Andrew Winter is the presenter of Selling Houses. *He has been a practising estate agent for over fifteen years and is a director of a thriving London practice – Lincoln Radley in Canary Wharf, E14. A seasoned house-mover himself, he now lives with his wife and two daughters in Kent.*

In each programme *Selling Houses* takes a home that won't sell and gives it real buyer appeal. And it works: after being given the *Selling Houses* treatment, homes that have failed to sell for months and months have buyers queuing up to make an offer. So far, all the properties featured in the series have been sold within a few weeks of going back on the market, and some have sold in just a few days.

As the presenter of the programme I have worked closely with the development of the series and this book. It has been a great opportunity to put my fifteen years' worth of experience as an estate agent – and my own frequent house moves – to good use. Over the years I have sold everything from small country cottages, barns for conversion and traditional semis to West End mansion-block flats and stylish contemporary city apartments. I also run an interiors business specialising in furnishing properties for the rental market and for sale, and I hope my wide-ranging experience has helped to create an interesting and informative series. In return I have really gained an insight into this fascinating subject, which affects almost all of us.

The programme sets to prove the theory that 'any house can be sold', no matter where it is or what it looks like. I believe very strongly that there is a buyer for every property. So often we discover that the way sellers present their homes has detracted buyers – a very costly mistake. It is my job in *Selling Houses* to show people how to make their homes appeal to buyers instead.

It is the role of the series to translate the experience of the participants into basic rules and advice that anyone could follow to maximise the saleability of their home. In this book we have tried to identify the key issues that will enable you to sell your home for the best price. The first of these golden rules is 'know your competition'. To do this you must understand the type of buyer you are seeking and what their list of priorities is likely to be. The second rule is 'know your local market'. Find out what other houses you are competing against locally and how you can make your home stand out from the crowd. And the third and final golden rule is 'clear your mind of personal debris', which is really all about

psychology. Your home and what you have in it says a lot about *you*, but what you want to do is to make it say a lot about *your buyer*.

This book is designed to help you transform your home so that you too can sell for the best possible price in the quickest possible time. Using the practical experience of the families in *Selling Houses*, we have taken a detailed look at each room in the house and given you ideas and tips, as well as case studies from the series that suggest projects that you could follow yourself. Many of these cost very little but will make your home instantly more appealing to your target buyer and possibly add thousands to its selling price.

If you follow our advice in the book, I have no doubt that you'll have no problem in selling your house for the price you want in no time at all. Happy selling!

Andrew Winter, January 2003

meet the families

8

Coco and Tak Peppas

Coco and Tak Peppas and their three boys live in an attractive Victorian three-bedroom terrace house in Charlton, an up-and-coming residential area close to Greenwich in southeast London. The house has been on the market for three months and they have had only six viewings and no offers. They are desperate to move. Both Coco and Tak work from home and with three growing boys, the family has outgrown the house. They have had an offer accepted on a larger house just round the corner and if they can't find a buyer quickly, they are likely to lose it.

The area is a big plus for Coco and Tak. House prices are less expensive than nearby Greenwich and the centre of Charlton has a villagey feel with plenty of trendy shops, bars and restaurants, and the smart shops in Blackheath aren't far away. With good transport links to the City and great schools, young professional families are flooding into the area.

Their house has plenty of period features, loads of space and a small south-facing garden, all big selling points with the couple's target market. But at the moment, the house isn't cutting the mustard with potential buyers. The hall has been replastered but is still undecorated and looks like a building site; the dining room has been turned into a bedroom; and the couple's bedroom is stuck in a hippy time warp. And the best room in the house, the front bedroom, isn't even a bedroom; it is being used as a workroom, where Coco makes her hats and the couple run their design business.

Nor have the couple sussed the competition. When Coco and Tak began selling their house, terraced houses in Charlton ranged from £220,000 for one with three bedrooms to £350,000 for four bedrooms. Just down the road a similar house in a better condition has just sold for £10,000 less than the £240,000 the Peppas family are asking. The Peppas have a job on their hands to get the price they need.

Dr Gary Wilbourne and Melanie Taylor

Dr Gary Wilbourne and Melanie Taylor have a two-bedroom first floor flat in Bedhampton near Portsmouth. It has been on the market for five months and is priced at £93,000. Only six people have been to see it and they have only had one very low offer. The couple need to move quickly because they have found their ideal home, a three-bedroom semi-detached house in a nearby street.

The flat has plenty going for it. It is in a good location between Portsmouth and Chichester and the village still seems quiet and peaceful. Inside, it is well proportioned with attractive period features. There is a good-sized living room with a large window overlooking the garden. Next to the living room there is a reasonably sized kitchen. Continuing down the main hall there is a small second bedroom, a bathroom, a separate shower room and a light and airy main bedroom. At the back there is a well established south-facing garden.

One of Gary and Melanie's biggest problems is their dog, a huge 140-pound Rottweiler called Henry. Gary and Melanie are probably unaware that Henry's smell pervades the whole flat and this is a big turn-off for buyers. Another is Gary's collection of guns and knives that is displayed on the hall walls and gives off a very unwelcoming and unfriendly message. The kitchen looks tired, dated and neglected; the spare room is piled high with junk including more of Gary's armoury collection; the carpets are worn and smell of their dog; and the shower room – a major selling point – is painted shocking pink, which does the room no favours.

There are few flats in Bedhampton which makes price comparisons difficult. When Gary and Melanie's flat is on the market, buyers with under £100,000 could buy a small two-bedroom house. However, a newly converted two-bedroom flat in a former village hall has just sold for £90,000; £3,000 less than Gary and Melanie are asking.

Ann Stolworthy

Ann Stolworthy and her two teenage daughters, who live in the pretty village of Alton in Staffordshire, are keen to move to a newly built four-bedroom detached house on a nearby development. But their plans are being thwarted because much to their surprise they can't sell their highly desirable seventeenth-century cottage. The cottage has been on the market now for six months at an asking price of £160,000, and has found no takers.

On the face of it, Ann and her daughters should have had no difficulty at all. Alton is a prosperous Staffordshire village with its own castle, lots of pretty stone cottages and quaint pubs. It has excellent schools and is attracting well-off families from nearby Derby and Stoke. With the local property market hotter than it has been for the last ten years, a pretty period cottage like Ann's ought to be a winner.

When you have lived in a home for a long time, it can be difficult to see it through the eyes of a buyer. Like many cottages, this one has an unusual layout and in Ann's case many of the spaces are unclearly defined, which buyers find confusing. Downstairs there is a small hallway. This leads to an L-shaped dining room that is also used as an office and a pet's bedroom. The main living room has high ceilings and French windows and should be the main selling point, but the décor is oppressive and there is too much clutter on the walls. A third reception room is a cross between a teenager's bedroom and a gym, complete with a sunbed and exercise bike. Upstairs there are three bedrooms and a bathroom. The main bedroom is not arranged to make the most of its best feature, the fireplace, and the bathroom has mouldy old tiles and a rotten old cork floor.

Cottages aren't easy to price because they are all unique. At the time Ann is selling, prices in North Staffordshire vary widely. Three-bedroom cottages are selling from around £140,000 and four-bedroom cottages from around £200,000. Five miles away in Cheddleton, a newly renovated four-bedroom, two-bathroom cottage has recently sold for £167,000, just £7,000 more than the price Ann is asking. Ann's cottage needs that 'newly converted' look if it is to sell.

Sean and Alison Blake

Sean and Alison Blake want to move from Latchington, a small village in a pretty part of Essex, to Milton Keynes, where Sean now works. Their three-bedroom semi-detached house has been on the market for nine months, and because they need every penny they can get to buy their new home in Milton Keynes, they are reluctant to drop the price below £125,000.

Latchington is a popular Essex village. It's got a good school, plenty of local amenities and a great local pub. For those things the village can't provide, it's just a half an hour drive to all the shops and restaurants in Chelmsford and with a train journey of just fifty minutes to London, it is popular with commuters. The house ought to be attractive to second-time buyers who need a larger house for a growing family.

The house is an ex-local authority semi built in the 1950s and like most former council properties in the area it is a good size. But it doesn't have a proper front door. Instead the entrance is through double patio doors into a playroom strewn with toys. Downstairs there is a narrow but functional dining room and a large bright sitting room, but the small kitchen is dark and gloomy. Adjoining the kitchen, there is a utility room housed in a con- servatory style extension. Upstairs there are three bedrooms and a bathroom. A major drawback is the lack of a toilet in the upstairs bathroom. As the target market is couples with young children, this is a major inconvenience. One of the biggest sell- ing points is the sun-filled 200-foot garden backing onto open fields.

11

This corner of Essex is dotted with picturesque villages full of cottages and small towns mainly made up of post-war housing. At the time Sean and Alison are selling, three-bedroom semi- detached houses sell for between £110,000 and £150,000. In the neighbouring town of South Woodham Ferrers, a similar semi, but with a larger kitchen and an upstairs toilet, recently sold for £125,000 – the price Alison and Sean want for their house. Without a major refit Sean and Alison will struggle to get the price they need so there's plenty for *Selling Houses* to work on.

Gay and Keith Keaveny

Gay and Keith Keaveny and their two teenage sons are opting for a complete change of lifestyle. They are hoping to sell their 1980s house in Croydon, south London, and move to the south of France where they have found an old five-bedroom farmhouse full of rural charm. But they are worried that their dreams may come to nothing because, in spite of dropping the asking price on their Croydon house by £30,000 to £300,000, the house remains unsold after seven months on the market.

Croydon is a popular town just ten miles south of London with plenty of employment opportunities. With excellent schools and a fast train service to London, it is popular with professional families. In this area, family houses normally sell within six to eight weeks, so it seems odd that

the Keavenys haven't yet found a buyer.

On the outside the house looks ideal. An imposing brick house with a pretty tile hung gable, double garage and a wide sweeping drive, this is most people's idea of the perfect executive home. The problem lies inside. The decoration is stuck in a 1980s time warp and needs to be dragged kicking and screaming into the twenty-first century. All the rooms downstairs are interlinked. The large living room with French windows flows into a good-sized dining room and on into a fitted kitchen, but each room is decorated in a different clashing style with old-fashioned floral wallpapers and contrasting borders, giving a very busy and distracting impression.

Upstairs there is a master bedroom with an en suite shower room, a gloomy family bathroom, two further children's rooms and a fourth bedroom that is being used as a study and needs to be reinstated as a bedroom. There is a 35-foot south-facing garden with space for entertaining, which is normally a big selling point.

At the time the Keavenys are selling, Croydon has a good supply of four-bedroom family homes priced at between £250,000 and £400,000. Most of them are older, period properties but a similar sized semi-detached house, which has the disadvantage of being close to a railway line, only went for £40,000 less than Gay and Keith are asking. But the real competition is from older houses with plenty of period details. A period house with bigger rooms and a huge garden in the next street has recently sold for just £13,000

Alicia McDonnell

city, and Castlefield with its canals has attracted many new bars and restaurants, adding to the neighbourhood's cool reputation. This is the lifestyle to which young professionals aspire and these are Alicia's target buyers.

Alicia's apartment is on the ground floor, but the back is partly underground. The flat is entered through attractive industrial-style black framed sliding doors with a decorated wood panel. It has a large combined living and dining room with a high ceiling and a wall of bare brick, but the room is unwelcoming and the furniture is not really appropriate to a smart, aspirational pad. There is a walk-through galley kitchen with stylish modern fittings, pale wood units and lots of stainless steel, but with no natural light, it seems dark and gloomy. At the back there are two bedrooms, a good-sized bathroom and separate toilet, but something is needed to disguise the underground feeling of these two rooms. At the front there is a small patio area that is totally unexploited.

In this area, there are lots of properties for sale and buyers are spoilt for choice. While Alicia is looking for a buyer, two-bedroom warehouse flat conversions in Castlefield are going for between £120,000 and £250,000. A one-bedroom flat in Alicia's block recently sold in a day. Although it had only one bedroom, in terms of space it was not much smaller than Alicia's. However, it had the advantage of being on the top floor with plenty of light and the original vaulted brick ceiling. It sold for £6,000 less than Alicia is asking which is worrying. Alicia seems to be asking a lot.

more than Gay and Keith's asking price.

For over a year, Alicia McDonnell has been trying to sell her ground floor warehouse-style flat in an attractive central Manchester development for £126,000. She has been renting it out and living elsewhere while she tries to sell it, but the flat is empty now. As well as costing Alicia money, the flat, like many tenanted properties, looks bare and uninviting. Alicia is now keen to speed up a sale because she has found a house she would like to buy in the leafy suburb of Didsbury.

Situated in the Castlefield area of Manchester, this is prime inner-city warehouse territory and very desirable. Other flats in Alicia's block shift within a month, so Alicia must be doing something wrong. More people are moving back into the centre of Manchester than any other British

Alan and Julie Johnson

14

Alan and Julie Johnson and their three children live in a four-bedroom 1930s Tudor-style semi-detached family house in Hornchurch in Essex. The couple used to own a newsagents shop but Alan is now an actor and Julie works in an office. They are moving to Lincolnshire so Julie can care for her ailing mother. They sold their newsagents business several months ago, hoping to sell their house soon afterwards. Their bank balance is telling them they must move quickly.

The house is located on the best road in the area and it is next to a London tube stop, and yet it has been on the market for four months. The asking price is £320,000 and the couple have had only eight viewings and no offers. Hornchurch is a real family area, with a good supply of large houses, pleasant parks, decent schools and an award-winning theatre.

Like a lot of 1930s houses, the layout of the Johnsons' house is fairly open plan, with two big reception rooms stretching from the front to the back of the house. There's also a bathroom and study by the front door. The kitchen is large for a 1930s house, having been extended to the rear. Upstairs, there is a master bedroom and three additional bedrooms, one of which features an en suite bathroom.

This is an ideal family house. It has plenty of space and a 120-foot garden. The problem is the house and its dated décor. Julie's family have owned the house for thirty years and it is stuck in a 1970s time warp and the spaces are all in a muddle.

The living room is dominated by an old-fashioned oak-panelled bar and a baby grand piano, and the beautiful original parquet floor is hidden under a swirly blue patterned carpet. The sitting room leads through two ugly red brick arches to a long narrow room with a built-in stone fireplace and an odd low stone shelf that runs much of the length of the room. In spite of the fact that this room is next to the kitchen, the couple use it as a living room rather than a dining room. The kitchen is in the rustic style. The units are a hotchpotch of open shelves built into low yellow brick walls.

The master bedroom is grim, with a worn, pale shagpile carpet and fitted cupboards that fill two of the room's walls.

The demand for family houses in the Johnsons' road outstrips supply. So why hasn't their house sold yet? Just a few doors down, a three-bedroom 1930s semi got an offer within a month of going on the market for £40,000 less than Alan and Julie's. Although it was smaller, it seems like much better value for money. And nearby, a four-bedroom 1930s house has attracted a lot of interest from buyers, even though it is on the market for £20,000 more than the Johnsons'.

Gill Davis

Gill Davis works as a beauty consultant for Estée Lauder and lives in a two-bedroom attic flat in a large period house in an elegant listed square in Surbiton, close to the river Thames in Surrey. Gill would like to move to a two-bedroom house with a garden, but her flat has been on the market for a year now. She is asking £185,000 and although she has had a massive thirty to forty viewings she has had only one offer – £180,000 – which she turned down.

Gill shouldn't be having such a problem. Surbiton with its riverside location, village atmosphere, trendy restaurants and fast train service to Waterloo station is attracting a lot of young buyers who are looking for one- and two-bedroom flats. The flat has a generously sized living room with great views, a separate kitchen with natural light and a range of fitted cupboards. Gill's master bedroom is also a good size with two skylight windows. There is a small second bedroom and a bathroom with another skylight that lets in the sunshine. And unusually for a flat this size there is plenty of storage space.

Around one in ten of Britain's house hunters are looking for flats like Gill's, so what is going wrong? Gill has lived in her flat for the last eight years, and in its present state it won't attract her target market – young professionals. They want a clean, contemporary look that they can move into straight away. Gill's flat looks tired, dated and clutter-strewn. There is too much oversized furniture in the sitting room and there is no dining area. The kitchen is soulless, and how has Gill coped all these years without a cooker? The main bedroom has no cupboards and Gill's clothes are left all over the place. The second bedroom has been turned into a junk room.

Surbiton is a happy hunting ground for flat dwellers. There are plenty of 'for sale' boards and most of these are for flats. Too many 'for sale' boards could indicate that people are queuing to move out, but in buzzing Surbiton it is a sign of a buoyant market. In Gill's square, flats have been known to sell in days or even hours, and buyers expect to pay between £170,000 and £270,000, depending on condition.

Two minutes away another two-bedroom conversion is on the market for £220,000. This is more expensive than Gill's but there is a living room with period features, a smart modern kitchen with a dining area, and a master bedroom with lots of wardrobe space. Another flat in a nearby 1920s block has a state-of-the-art kitchen, a clutter-free sitting room, a spacious bedroom and luxurious bathrooms. Both these properties prove that in Surbiton there is a market for flats with smart modern décor and people are happy to pay the price to get the quality they want. If Gill manages to improve the look of her home, on the evidence of these other flats, she may even be able to up her asking price.

Mark and Miriam Krepka

Mark and Miriam Krepka live in a modern four-bedroom detached house in a small cul-de-sac close to the centre of Sandy, a small market town not far from Bedford. The house first went on the market in January 2002 with an asking price of £249,950. There have been only eight viewings and the couple turned down one offer of £220,000, but have now cut the asking price to £239,950.

Mark wants to move closer to the computer shop that he owns in Rushden in Northamptonshire, but he is having difficulty selling his house because there is hot competition from nearby new developments. Houses in these developments are not much more expensive than Mark's, but buyers have the added luxury of being able to choose from a wide range of the most up-to-the-minute flooring and kitchen and bathroom fittings.

Mark and Miriam's house is in a cul-de-sac of just twelve houses and has a south-facing garden. It has an entrance hall, a useful study and downstairs cloakroom, and a large living room with sliding patio doors onto the garden. There is a separate dining room, a large kitchen-cum-breakfast room, a master bedroom with an en suite bathroom, three further bedrooms, a family bathroom, and a double garage.

This is an ideal family house – but there can be a problem with nearly-new houses. Unless you can give them a bit of pizzazz they can quickly look dated and will appeal neither to buyers who prefer period houses nor buyers who like new homes. And pizzazz is what Mark and Miriam's house is lacking. The first rule when selling a house is usually to clear out the clutter. Unusually, this house is absolutely devoid of clutter. What is needed here is an infusion of style and personality. The living room is bare and clinical and dominated by an ugly tartan, leatherette suite. The dining room is clearly defined with a table and chairs but the patterned lace net curtains and the curtains with floral borders and tiebacks look as if they came from a retirement home. The kitchen is a nice big room with pale coloured kitchen cabinets, but the blue colour scheme and the dull lace curtains make the room seem cold and dated.

Lots of new houses are going up in Sandy, which has become a thriving centre for the service industry. This is a problem for Mark and Miriam whose house is competing on price with a plentiful supply of these developments, and there is not much difference in price between these new houses and their own. Five minutes away, a new detached house is on the market for £270,000, but even more worryingly, there are other four-bedroom new houses in the town which are on the market for £242,000, just £2,000 more than the Krepkas'. Their target market is young families looking for a modern house, but to get the price they want, their house must look like a show house.

Sandra and Geoffrey Coleman

Health service manager Geoffrey Coleman spends three hours a day commuting to his job in Oxfordshire. His wife, Sandra, would like to see more of him, so they have decided to move closer to his job. The couple and their four children live in a 1930s four-bedroom detached house with plenty of character features, half a mile from the centre of High Wycombe, an attractive Buckinghamshire market town.

The house has been on the market for seven months for £240,000. They have had at most eight viewings and no offers. The house should sell quickly. It is in a good area with views out to the lovely Chiltern hills. It is within walking distance of a primary school, the station and town centre, and borders on the smart Wycombe Hill area.

Geoffrey and Sandra need to get a good price because they are moving to an expensive rural area. The house is double-glazed throughout, has two well-proportioned reception rooms, a large kitchen-breakfast room and a downstairs toilet. Upstairs, there is a master bedroom with a wood laminate floor, a good-sized second bedroom, two further bedrooms, and a fitted bathroom. Outside, there is a 40-foot garden, a garage and a driveway with off-street parking for two cars, a useful bonus in a street with parking restrictions.

But the Colemans may be putting off buyers because they are turned off by their child-centred home. The family doesn't have a television and their front room is used as a music room and play area. The piano dominates the room and there are toys everywhere. The children need some-where to study at home, and the back reception room has not one but two computers.

The surrounding streets are a mix of Victorian and 1930s houses and prices for three- and four-bedroom family houses range widely from £200,000 to £290,000, but there are significant differences in quality. Just a few streets away there is a highly attractive family house on sale for £230,000, £10,000 less than the Colemans'. This house has two well-decorated and nicely furnished reception rooms, a big utility room and lots of original features, but only three bedrooms.

A four-bedroom house in the same area has recently sold for £290,000, which is £50,000 more than the Colemans' house, but it has two smart living rooms and the added bonus of a cellar, conservatory and a study.

what you need to know

Selling houses is no different from selling baked beans, soap powder, Gucci handbags or top-of-the-range sports cars. Whatever you are selling, the same rules of marketing apply. Even though your house is special to you, don't make the mistake of thinking that it will necessarily appeal to anyone else. To make a successful sale for the most amount of money, in the least amount of time, you must start thinking and acting like a salesman.

When you are getting ready to sell your house, don't skip on the preparation. As Andrew says, before you do anything else there are three golden rules of marketing that you must master. The first is know your buyer; the second is know the competition; the third is clear your mind of personal debris.

know your buyer

We are not talking here about sending out extensive questionnaires or holding focus groups. But you do need to sit down and think carefully about your house and who it is likely to appeal to. Look at the area, local house prices, your neighbours, the local schools, the shops, bars and restaurants, open spaces, and transport links. These are all key factors buyers take into account when they go house hunting.

It might seem obvious but if you live in an area of spacious three- and four- bedroom houses with good local schools, your buyer is most likely to be a family with children. A flat in an inner-city area with good transport links close to trendy bars and restaurants is likely to appeal to young professionals. While a small cottage in a quiet village is most likely to appeal to a retired couple.

But it is surprising how wrong people can get it. Coco and Tak Peppas are selling a spacious three-bedroom house in Charlton with great family appeal. Except no one crossing the threshold gets the message because the dining room has been turned into a bedroom and the most beautiful room in the house – the front bedroom – has been turned into a chaotic workroom.

Remember most buyers lack imagination. Faced with a house without a clear message, most find it impossible to imagine what it will look like once they have imposed their own taste. When you know who your buyer is likely to be, you can set about making sure that they are

to sell your house

opposite First- 19
time buyers tend
to choose flats.

left Many
retired couples
want a bungalow
to move to.

presented with a vision that will allow them to make that leap of imagination.

Style also conveys a powerful message. Alicia McDonnell's warehouse flat in Manchester ought to appeal to young professionals for whom warehouse living in the inner city, close to bars and restaurants, is the height of chic. But Alicia's flat is a real turn-off. The flat is full of hand-me-downs, while our young professionals are dreaming of furniture by B & B Italia.

A quick tour of the local estate agents windows tells you a lot about style. Estate agents only display the houses with the best-looking, most fashionable interiors. But different styles attract different people, so it is important to know

what kind of look is selling in your kind of home, in your kind of area. In Alicia's case she needs to find a clean and contemporary look for her warehouse flat. But this is not a look that is universal. For example, in affluent areas of family houses, comfortable soft furnishings, lavish curtains, and thick pile carpets might be the look that sells houses, and family houses decorated out of character along strictly minimalist lines might not sell easily at all.

Remember too, that if a house doesn't have immediate buyer appeal, most buyers won't even consider it. Even if a house is selling at a hefty discount to its more desirable neighbours, many buyers aren't clever enough to work out whether it would cost less to buy the house and upgrade it than buy one that is already to their taste – and many just don't want the hassle of the extra work once they have moved in.

know the competition

Getting the price right is absolutely crucial to getting a fast and profitable sale, which is why it is worth spending some time investigating the local opposition before you call in any estate agents for a valuation. Put too high a price on your house and it will languish unsold, and a house that remains on the market for more than a few months will struggle to find a buyer. Put too low a price on your house, and you may have the buyers queuing up, but you will always wonder if you could have sold it for more.

Valuation is both an art and a science and unless you have looked at the competition it is hard to judge whether you are asking the right price. In this country, houses are usually valued according to how many bedrooms they have. So in any area, an estate agent can quote you a range of prices for, say, two-bedroom flats, three-bedroom terrace houses, or four-bedroom detached houses.

A more scientific way of valuing houses is to look at the price per square foot, or if you prefer metric, price per square metre. This is how homes are valued almost everywhere else in the world, and property details in Europe and the United States invariably contain this figure.

If you want to work out the value of your house using this yardstick, try grabbing a handful of property details of houses similar to yours from your local estate agents. Many estate agents now include floor plans and include a figure for the amount of space in the house. From these figures you can work out the price per square foot or square metre. This is a useful method of finding out which houses look cheap and which

expensive, and if there is a house very similar to your own, it will provide the best guide to how much you should be asking. If no figure is given in the details, you can get a rough guide by calculating the floor area of each room and adding 10 per cent for halls, stairs and landings.

However, valuation is not strictly scientific. There are other factors that affect price. For example, end-of-terrace houses are less secure, so less desirable, and can be cheaper. A property on a main road will be cheaper than the same house on a quieter road. A south- or west-facing garden is more desirable than one facing east or north. A house with a clean, modern kitchen and bathroom will always be worth more than one where these crucial features need replacing. A house with period features, such as the original fireplaces, cornicing, panelled doors and sash windows will always be worth more than one where most of these features have been ripped out.

Armed with all this information, you should now be in a strong position to get your house valued. Estate agents don't charge for valuations,

right Get ideas about what sells from the photographs in estate agents' windows.

and it is a good idea to get valuations from at least three agents: you may be surprised at how different they are. Don't be tempted to go with the agent who says he can get the best price for you if this is way out of line with your own research. Instead choose an agent who is enthusiastic about your house, offers sound advice about presentation and seems keen to sell it, as well as being realistic about the price.

Most of the *Selling Houses* families failed to sell their houses quickly because they were slightly overvalued and they hadn't done their research. The Keaveny family in Croydon are forced to cut the price on their 1980s four-bedroom family house with its dated interior by £30,000 to £300,000. Croydon has plenty of three- and four-bedroom family houses, and the main competition was from period properties with much more spacious rooms. Disconcertingly, one such house in the next street had just sold for only £13,000 more than the Keavenys' house. They were obviously pushing their luck.

If Coco and Tak Peppas had done their research, they would have found that a house, similar to their own, but in better condition, has just sold for £230,000: £10,000 less than they are asking for their house. That should have set the alarm bells ringing.

Mark and Miriam Krepka were originally asking £242,000 for their four-bedroom modern house in Sandy in

> **Andrew says:** Find out the most a home like yours has sold for in the same area. If the asking price is wrong, you've no chance of selling your house.

Bedfordshire. The house was competing with lots of new properties on nearby developments where four-bedroom houses were available for £245,000. As a result Mark and Miriam's house had languished unsold for a year and they were forced to cut the price to £239,950.

clear your mind of personal debris

It can be hard for sellers to look at a much-loved house with a critical eye. You might have agonised for months over the choice of colour for your sitting room walls but not everyone will share your taste for Tuscan terracotta, or rag-rolled yellow, or decorative borders. And that wall full of family portraits or artful displays of treasures collected on your travels might bring a warm glow to your heart, but they mean absolutely nothing to your buyer, and could even be a huge turn-off.

below Compare house prices by using the information in estate agents' details.

21

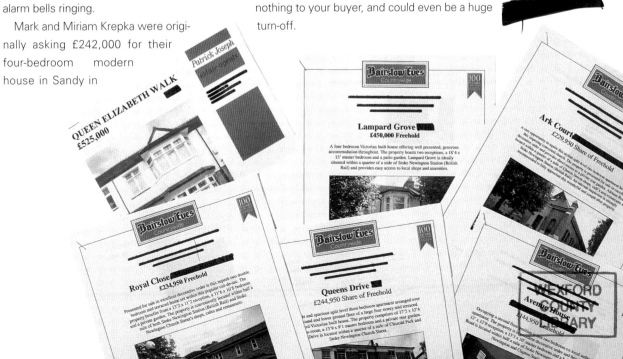

Gay Keanevy looks hurt when she is told that the large school portraits of her children on prominent display on the dining room wall in her house in Croydon have to go. And Gary Wilbourne and Melanie Taylor seem surprised by the news that Gary's collection of knives and guns might be giving off a needlessly aggressive message, or that the smell of their huge Rottweiler, Henry, pervades the whole flat. Melanie is critical of the coir carpet that replaces her existing carpet. She calls it hideous and says Henry will rip it to pieces. In fact, the buyers love the new carpet, and Melanie won't be there long enough for her dog to destroy it.

Alison Blake hates the Venetian blinds in the conservatory part of her new kitchen/diner, which give the room a contemporary look. What Melanie and Alison forget is that these changes are being made to attract buyers. They are not there for their own benefit so their taste doesn't come into it.

Sandra Coleman resists the idea that her child-centred lifestyle may be putting off buyers. In the Coleman household the four children rule the roost. Their toys and possessions are strewn throughout the house, but the family is uncomfortable with attempts to bring some order to their chaos, even though the family is only being asked to rein in their children's exuberance and creativity for the time it takes to sell the house.

Sellers like Melanie, Alison and Sandra find it hard to accept that not everyone shares their taste, or lifestyle, and that a successful seller is someone who can see their house through the eyes of a buyer.

the basics

Every home is different, and what sells one house may not sell another. But there are still some basic ground rules that work like magic in almost all homes, whether they are large, medium or small. Before putting your home on the market, use the following basics as a check list. These tips are always followed by people who successfully sell their houses and they come up time and time again on *Selling Homes*.

First impressions count. Tidy up front gardens, getting rid of dead pot plants and rubbish bins. If the front door needs a fresh coat of paint, then paint it, and if the brass needs a polish, polish it. If you are selling a flat and the communal areas look dirty and scruffy, approach the other owners and suggest a facelift. If they refuse, think about paying for the hallway up to your own flat to

22 **below** Keep rooms and windows sparkling clean.

be repainted at your own expense. Make sure that any outside lights are working. There is nothing more scary than a dark porch or drive. Gravel drives should be thick and crunchy and weed free. If your porch has been boxed in, is this an advantage or a disadvantage? Will your prospective buyer like the idea of somewhere to put the pot plants in winter and the dirty wellies, or would they prefer to see the porch returned to its original state?

Tidy up. This might seem very obvious, but estate agents will tell you that they are constantly surprised at how many people expect to sell their houses with last night's dirty dishes in the sink and clothes strewn all over the bedrooms. So clear away the washing up, hide those clothes drying in the bathroom, hang up your dresses and suits and fold up your T-shirts and knickers and put them back in the chest of drawers.

Spring clean and keep it clean. Prepare your house for the hordes of buyers who will see it by giving it a top to bottom spring clean – and then vow to keep it that way. A clean and tidy house gives the impression of a much-loved house. And don't neglect the windows. Anyone viewing a house on a sunny day will immediately notice if the windows are dirty.

Clear away the clutter. It may mean a lot to you, but to a buyer it is just rubbish. Depersonalise your house by tidying away your bits and pieces, clearing kitchen work surfaces, mantelpieces and dressing tables. You can then make displays with just a few well-chosen objects. Rationalise the storage of books, CDs and videos. Take any that you are unlikely to read, listen to or watch again to your local charity shop, and arrange what's left neatly. A good tip is to arrange paperback books by the colours on their spine. There is nothing more cheerful than a row of brightly coloured books.

Don't neglect routine maintenance.
A dripping pipe or a leaking gutter can cause damage and might put off a potential buyer. Give your house a thorough check. Are there any damp patches that need dealing with; is there moss growing where a down pipe leaked; is there a build-up of limescale from a leaking tap? None of these is a serious problem, but you must put it right.

23

Depersonalise. Clear away stuff which gives too much away about your personality and family, such as evidence of hobbies, sporting activities and family photographs. Buyers need to imagine their own lives in your house; they don't need to know the details of your life.

Keep pets at bay. Animal hair and animal smells are a big minus. Not everyone loves animals and some buyers may even be allergic to them. When buyers come round, get someone to take the dog for a walk and put the cats in the garden.

above A messy, untidy room is a real turn-off.

24

above Subtle lighting makes a big difference.

Neutral colours work best. *Cream, pale beige and even magnolia are light, bright and fresh. They create a blank canvas on which buyers can project their own fantasies. Dark colours and bright shades are too personal. Buyers will either love them or loathe them, which means you are restricting the number of potential purchasers.*

Kitchens and bathrooms sell houses. This doesn't mean spending thousands on new fittings. Simple measures such as painting dated dark wooden units in the kitchen, replacing worn tiling in the bathroom or putting down new flooring can make all the difference. Installing a power shower in the bathroom won't cost a fortune but is a big attraction, especially for younger buyers. Then add well-chosen accessories, such as

attractive stainless steel storage containers or a designer kettle or espresso machine in the kitchen. In the bathroom, a new shower curtain, loads of fluffy white towels and a selection of top-of-the-range toiletries will add instant appeal.

Take care of the lighting. *Lighting can help create a feeling of comfort and intimacy. In sitting rooms and bedrooms, table and standard lamps work better than overhead lighting or wall lights. Get them wired into the main light switches so that you can turn them on and off as you leave the room. This will impress buyers who view your house for the first time after dark or when the weather is gloomy.*

Make sure each room has a clearly defined purpose. Studies that double as bedrooms, bedrooms that double as gyms, and halls that look like playrooms just confuse buyers. Define the purpose of each room, keeping an eye on your likely buyer and how they will use the house.

Buy fresh flowers. *Throw out all tired looking pot plants even if you think they might recover. Invest instead in regular supplies of fresh flowers or flowering pot plants such as azaleas and cyclamens that are only designed to have a limited life. Flowers add a touch of luxury to any room. A simple arrangement of a single variety, with a strong colour tied into your colour scheme, works better than complicated bunches of mixed flowers of the variety commonly sold on garage forecourts.*

Tidy up the garden. You may be a keen gardener, but a garden that looks as if it might be a lot of work can be a disadvantage. Make sure the garden is tidy and looks low-maintenance. Cut the lawn, mend the fence, cut back unruly shrubs, give the patio a scrub and clear up any leaves. And if there isn't a sitting-out and barbecue area, create one.

Selling an empty house. *Selling an empty house can be surprisingly difficult. The philosophy behind clearing away your clutter and depersonalising it is to allow your buyers to imagine their own lives unfolding in your house. This can be almost impossible if the house is empty and cleared of furniture. If you can, attempt to create the appearance of a lived-in house. Either leave it furnished or hire furniture for the purpose.*

Know when to break the rules. Once you have followed all these rules, take a close look at what you have achieved. If it looks just too cold and impersonal, now is the time to break the rules. Think about adding a splash of colour or a few personal touches. For example, you could think of painting just one wall in an exciting fashionable colour or add a few glamorous velvet or satin cushions to the sofa in the sitting room.

left Bright accent colours give neutrally decorated rooms a real lift.

25

Andrew says: Don't expect to sell your house easily. Be prepared for some really hard work.

the economics of making money out of your house

Most people do up their homes not because they want to sell them but because they want somewhere comfortable and stylish to live. Having a beautiful home is now a major status symbol; it is as important as driving the right car or taking holidays in the smartest resorts.

Buying a home is the biggest investment that most people make and even though you may intend to stay put for many years, it is still important to be aware of which improvements are likely to make you money; which will recover the investment; and which may not be worth doing at all financially, but which you may decide to do anyway because they will bring you pleasure.

Of course, there are other people who make a living out of buying a home, doing it up and then moving on to the next project. For these property developers, the arithmetic of doing up houses is particularly important.

A recent survey by the Abbey National, one of Britain's biggest mortgage lenders, revealed a nation addicted to home improvement. According to the Abbey National, the three improvements most likely to make you money are adding an extension, a loft conversion or a garage. Improvements which are likely to pay for themselves include fitting a new kitchen, installing central heating and putting in double glazing or replacement windows. Those where

Andrew says: When you sell your car, you clean it and repair any damage in order to get the best price. So why don't you do the same with your house?

duty thresholds, think very carefully before doing costly improvements if this puts your house into a higher stamp duty band. For example, if your house is currently worth £249,000, there is no point in spending £20,000 on putting in a new loft room, if it means the value of your house increases to £269,000. If you had to sell the house this would increase the stamp duty bill from £2,490 to £8,070, an extra £5,580. Most people would be reluctant to pay the extra tax. It could mean you would be forced to accept an offer below the stamp duty threshold and you would have lost money.

Do your research. *Look at the most common improvements that are carried out in your area and how much they add to the value of the house before taking any decision. Local estate agents will be able to give you a rough idea of which improvements will make you money. House prices can vary from road to road and it could be that a roof extension, say, in one road makes financial sense, but doesn't in another street half a mile away. In some areas there will be a price ceiling for your type of house, with buyers reluctant to pay a premium for even the most beautiful features.*

Avoid improvements that unbalance a house. Extending a house can leave it feeling unbalanced. It might suit your needs, but it is always important to think about who will eventually buy your house. For example,

opposite It doesn't always make sense to convert a bedroom in to a bathroom.

left A conservatory can add value but not at the expense of the garden.

27

you won't recoup your investment include building a swimming pool, landscaping your garden, turning your bedroom into a bathroom and stripping wooden floors.

Surveys like this are useful guides to what can make you money, but they are by no means infallible. It is also important to do your own research because local factors can have a big impact on the equation.

Stamp duty. Stamp duty can have a distorting effect on house prices. There is no stamp duty to pay on homes selling for less than £60,000. On houses selling for between £60,000 and £250,000, the rate is normally 1 per cent; on houses selling for between £250,000 and £500,000 the rate jumps to 3 per cent, and on those selling for £500,000 plus the rate is 4 per cent. If your house is valued at just below one of the stamp

28 **right** A good, modern kitchen will sell a house.

a house with a conservatory that takes up most of the garden may not be as attractive to buyers as a larger garden, where the children can kick a football. A fifth bedroom in the loft might have given you extra space, but without the addition of an extra bathroom, it may be just one too many bedrooms. You might like the idea of acres of living space, but think carefully before you create a large living area out of two smaller rooms. Many families prefer a formal sitting room that is kept for the grown-ups and a separate playroom for the children; while more traditional older couples like to have a separate dining room.

Make improvements that enhance the period character of a house. *Period features are generally big selling points. Houses with the original wooden sash windows will always sell better than those with replacement plastic windows. You are better off spending your money overhauling the original windows rather than putting in replacement modern ones. If you are determined to put in double glazing, either buy secondary glazing, which is fitted inside the house, or invest in new wooden sash windows with double glazed panes. Spending time and money on restoring* decorative cornicing and old fireplaces is money well spent. Salvage yards are a good place to look if you want to reinstate the original panel doors or find some replacement stained glass for your front door.

Pay attention to kitchens and bathrooms. You may dream of a state-of-the-art German freestanding kitchen but your budget probably doesn't stretch that far. However, it remains a fact that a good-looking modern kitchen and a simple bathroom with a white suite and a power shower will make it much easier to sell your house quickly, even if it only recoups your investment. The big furniture stores and do-it-yourself chains all sell reasonably priced, well-designed kitchens and bathrooms.

If you are making major improvements use an architect or surveyor. If you are thinking of pulling down structural walls or building an extension, hiring an architect or surveyor might save you money in the long run. You may need planning permission, or if you are doing work that involves your next door neighbour's wall, there will be party wall awards to sort out. And if your building is listed or in a conservation area you may need listed building consent. Whenever structural work is involved you will need permission from the local building inspector who works for your council. Without the right consents you may have difficulty selling your house because solicitors worth their salt will want proof that any works have been carried out in a structurally safe way. An architect or surveyor will make sure that you have all the right permits in place. If they are local they will have the added advantage of being able to recommend well-respected local builders.

Think about investing in cutting-edge design. Hiring an architect to design something unique and special can add value to your house. As a nation we are becoming increasingly design conscious. There are a growing number of magazines devoted to interior design and most of them are full of enticing pictures of homes that have been transformed with the help of an architect. They are trained to come up with fresh ideas, and it is this different slant on a problem that could make you a mint. But be careful. Using an architect need not cost a fortune, but they do have a reputation for getting carried away, so it is important to establish a budget at the outset. Also, be aware that cutting-edge design will only add value in areas where there is a demand for it. People in affluent, trendy and sophisticated areas will happily pay a premium for something different. It is likely to sink like a lead balloon in the back streets of a run-down industrial town, or in a traditional English village.

below Bathrooms are a big selling point too.

29

the
hall

the hall

32

It's a cliché, but true: first impressions really do count, and after the front garden, front door and – if you live in a flat – the communal areas, it is the hall that sets the scene for the whole house. Unfortunately, not every house is blessed with a beautiful hall. In many houses it is a long thin corridor with little to commend it and making the most of it can be an uphill struggle.

tips

Make sure your bell works. Bell or knocker, it doesn't matter, but make sure that you can hear it wherever you are in the house and, if it is a bell, it can be heard from the outside too. There is nothing more unsettling for viewers than not knowing if you have heard them arrive.

Watch the locks. It is good to be security conscious but you don't want to give potential buyers the idea that you might be worried about crime levels in the area. When buyers call, open the door promptly – don't leave them standing on the doorstep while you spend a couple of minutes unlocking the door and releasing the chain.

Invest in a large doormat. People are often nervous entering a house for the first time. They worry they may be trailing mud and dirt into your spotlessly clean house. A nice large coir mat – admittedly, not a thing of great beauty – puts people at their ease. Getting it set into the floor or carpet is a neat solution.

Create the feeling of space. Halls are often used as a general storage area for all sorts of things. No house hunter wants to be greeted with an obstacle course. Put the bikes in the garden shed or chain them to the lamp post in the road; tidy away those piles of coats. You could leave one or two items of designer clothing artfully arranged on a coat rack, but if you don't have any it is better to leave the coat rack bare or dispense with it entirely. If the hall is narrow remove the hall table or think about replacing it with a small shelf for keys and post.

Don't ignore the lighting. The lighting in halls and on landings is often ignored. Most are lit from ceiling pendants which can give a harsh and unappealing light. Table lamps placed on the hall shelf or, if there is room for one, the hall table, give a much softer, more intimate feel. The other alternative is to invest in unusual pendant lights that make a statement. Giant paper lampshades are cheap and cheerful. More expensive alternatives such as Moroccan-style star lanterns or Scandinavian folded paper shades can be taken with you when you move.

Andrew says: Make sure your front door is immaculate and well painted. It is the first contact with your home.

Create an interesting vista. *A glimpse through to one of the rooms off the hall creates interest and is a better alternative to a dull view up the stairs. It could be a tempting sight of the designer kitchen or a lush view of the garden at the height of summer. But don't create too much confusion. One vista is enough, so keep other doors closed, with the rooms behind waiting to be discovered.*

Make the most of original features. Stained glass windows and tessellated floors are original features that are strong selling points and add interest to a hall. Unless they are in poor condition, display them, and if they need minor repairs, get them done.

The effort could all be wasted. *Getting your front door, bell and locks sorted will all be a waste of time if you have ignored your front garden. Make sure the hedges are trimmed and the flowerbeds are weeded. Get rid of any rubbish and dead plants and hide the dustbins and recycling bins. Invest in some smart window boxes for the windowsills or a couple of matching pot plants to place each side of the front door. Pyramids of box or standard bay trees may be expensive but give a good impression and you can take them to your next home. And make sure there is good lighting between the street and your front door, especially if buyers will be arriving after dark.*

Use the hall flooring to give the house a unified feel. *You can improve the flooring in a home for less than £500 but this can add as much as £5,000 to the eventual selling price. Create a unified flooring scheme by running the same flooring from the hall into the main living rooms. This helps create a feeling of spaciousness.*

Create interest. As a general rule a surfeit of pictures gives out too much of a personal statement about the current owners. However, a drab hall can be lifted with the careful use of prints or arty photos. Arrange them in a well-defined pattern or place at least three themed pictures – for example large flower prints or art deco travel posters – in a row on the wall.

Choose the right flooring. This is a question of knowing your market. Young buyers like stripped wood or laminate wood-effect floors, while families appreciate hard-wearing surfaces such as coir, sisal and seagrass. Older couples like carpet, although these should be plain and not patterned as these make spaces look small.

Work with the flooring you have. *Carpets can be cleaned; do it yourself with hired equipment, or pay professionals to do it for you. If the floorboards are in a good state, you can hire a sander and vanish them, or you can just give them a quick rub down with sandpaper and then paint them with hard-wearing floor paint.*

modernising a dated hall

right An overloaded coat rack dominates the Keaveny's hall.

below The hallway leads to an uninspiring staircase.

the problem

Gay and Keith Keaveny's modern house in Croydon needs bringing up to date, erasing all signs of its dated 1980s décor. The hall is cluttered with keys, coats and dog leads, and to get into the living room you stumble past a storage bench. The downstairs rooms are all linked and need a much more unified approach.

the solution

Create a clean, bright and modern first impression. The bench goes into storage along with much of the couple's other furniture. Wood laminate flooring is installed in the hall and is run through all the downstairs rooms to achieve a much-needed feeling of unity. The quality of the lighting is improved with some bright, modern-looking halogen lights.

> The downstairs rooms are all linked and need a more unified approach

cost:
£85

a hall that looks like a building site

far left Coco and Tak, ready to cover the plaster once and for all.

left The Peppas' hall and landing look unfinished, creating a bad first impression.

the problem

Coco and Tak Peppas have replastered the hall and landing and prepared all the woodwork in their Victorian terrace house in south-east London, but the plaster is still bare and the woodwork hasn't been repainted. It looks like a building site and creates a dreadful first impression.

the solution

Redecorate. The bare plaster and woodwork in the hall and landing are painted in a neutral shade of off-white. The hall floor has been sanded, but the dirty carpet on the stairs and landing is replaced with new sisal covering that gives the hall a contemporary look. Coco and Tak are an artistic couple with a huge collection of interesting paintings. A selection, including some portraits of their children, are hung on the walls to add interest to both the hall and landing.

it creates a dreadful first impression

cost:
£575
of which the sisal carpet cost £425

turning a playroom back into a hall

the problem

Sean and Alison Blake's house in Latchington in Essex has no proper front door. Instead you enter a large hall through patio doors, which Andrew Winter describes as one of the weirdest front doors he has ever seen. The area is strewn with toys and looks more like a playroom than a hall. There is no time to replace the patio doors with a proper front door and a window, but at the very least it is essential that the space is redefined as a hall rather than a children's play area.

the solution

Create a hall. The room is painted a fresh shade of cream and the toys are stored behind a newly installed folding screen. The children's blackboard is removed from the back door, and a large pot plant is bought to add a touch of interest to what is a relatively large space.

above Unusually, the Blake's have a patio window instead of a front door.

opposite Andrew and Alison get to work.

the area is strewn with toys and looks more like a playroom than a hall

cost: £206

chapter
four
the
kitchen

the kitchen

Kitchens and bathrooms are huge selling points, and a good kitchen can clinch a quick sale, which is why getting your kitchen right is the number one priority when you start thinking about selling your house. And remember, kitchen design moves fast. A kitchen that looked cutting edge five years ago can easily look dated now, but this doesn't mean spending a fortune on a new one. Instead there are plenty of simple, cheap tricks that you can use to give yesterday's kitchen a contemporary designer look.

Not all buyers want the same thing out of a kitchen, so think too about what your buyer is likely to want. If yours is a family house, it will need to be a multi-purpose room. These days, family life often revolves around the kitchen. It is a place where the children play, do their homework, where small businesses get started and, most importantly, it is the place where the family gathers at meal times. As well as being fashionable, family kitchens must also be spacious, practical, hardworking, welcoming and cosy.

Busy professionals may not spend much time in the kitchen. They may not know the difference between a fan oven and a grill, and their idea of cooking is popping an occasional ready meal into the microwave, but that doesn't mean you can palm them off with a tired and dated look. For these buyers a smart designer kitchen is a must-have status symbol.

The kitchen is the most expensive room in the house and if it needs work, buyers will be put off by the thought of the money they will need to spend on installing a new one. A clean, spacious and practical kitchen is your biggest selling point. A poor kitchen can make an otherwise lovely house difficult to sell because buyers lack the imagination to see that updating it doesn't necessarily mean spending big bucks.

tips

Paint old-fashioned units. Dark wooden units can make a kitchen look gloomy. Think about painting the units a pale, neutral colour. This lightens and freshens up a dated kitchen, giving the impression of space.

Replace unit doors. Most units come in standard sizes so it is easy to find new doors that fit. Or you could ask a carpenter to run up some new doors out of painted MDF.

Replace work surfaces. A grubby, scratched work surface with burn marks should be replaced. A new work surface doesn't have to cost a fortune, and can be cut to size and easily fitted. They come in a huge range of different materials, colours and styles, and can give old units a completely new lease of life.

Scrap an old-fashioned cooker. Large freestanding stainless steel range-style cookers are all the rage, but old-fashioned freestanding cookers are old hat. To make your kitchen look up-to-date, rip out the old cooker and install a fitted oven and hob instead.

Fit new handles. *Fitting new handles can transform the look of kitchen units. Use simple stainless steel or brushed steel handles for a contemporary feel.*

Paint plinths. Paint the plinths at the bottom of units in a dark colour. This gives the impression that the floor disappears under the units, creating a sense of space.

Modernise the lighting. *Replace old-fashioned ceiling lights or spotlights with smart halogen lights, and think about placing some directional lighting under wall cabinets over work surfaces. Fit dimmer switches if the kitchen is multi-functional. Dinner party guests do not want to eat in the glaring light needed for cooking.*

Create a dedicated eating area. If your kitchen is large enough, create a dedicated dining area to create the feeling of a real family room. Wide, spacious kitchens can be separated from the dining area with a breakfast bar, but if your kitchen is narrow, a counter jutting out into the room will make it look smaller.

Replace flooring. *Replace worn and grimy flooring with a value-for-money vinyl or wood laminate floor.*

Clear the work surfaces. *Work surfaces should be cleared of cookery books, pots and pans, and other cooking paraphernalia for an uncluttered look.*

Accessorise your kitchen. Invest in a set of smart storage jars, and a good-looking fruit bowl kept topped up with an inviting display of fresh fruit.

Spring clean. *Kitchens are absolute grease magnets, so give every surface a thorough clean and use a grouting pen if the grouting between the tiles looks dirty.*

Bin the bin. Dustbins and pedal bins in the kitchen are off-putting. Install a bin inside a cupboard, and make sure it smells fresh by cleaning it out with bleach.

Think about your buyer. *A city kitchen for a young professional needs to look ultra modern. A family kitchen needs to feel more cosy. If your revamped family kitchen looks too neutral add some touches of colour with curtains or a roman blind and co-ordinated table cloth, but don't overdo it.*

41

Andrew says: Have a sniff. If your home smells unpleasant, sort it out. Buyers and nasty niffs don't go.

creating a family kitchen

below A light, bright conservatory is wasted as a utility room.

right The kitchen is just too small to appeal to a family.

the problem

Young families are the most likely buyers of Sean and Alison Blake's house but the small, dark and poky kitchen is little more than a walk-in larder and is working against them.

the solution

Create a smart kitchen diner that appeals to families by linking the existing lean-to conservatory with the kitchen. This is an imaginative solution to a difficult problem.

The existing lean-to conservatory is tacked on to the back of the house. It is used as a storage and utility room and because it is not double glazed it can only be used in summer. In order to integrate the conservatory with the house, the door and the window between the kitchen and the conservatory are removed. A breakfast bar with smart bar stools is installed in the conservatory. This is achieved by lowering the wall where the window was removed. After checking with the building regulations the conservatory is re-roofed with double-glazed units to make it cosy in winter. The washer-dryer is replumbed and repositioned in new units to make way for the breakfast bar.

cost:
£975
including labour

left The old utility room becomes a bright eating space in a family kitchen.

below White units and a hatch to allow light in make the kitchen feel more spacious.

The kitchen and the conservatory are painted in a unifying shade of off-white and the dark kitchen units are painted white, which lightens the previously gloomy galley space. Smart, full-length contemporary venetian blinds are fitted on two of the conservatory windows to create a sense of enclosure while maintaining views of the attractive garden, which is a big selling point. Opening up and linking the kitchen with the conservatory creates the necessary sense of space that families look for in a kitchen.

the kitchen and the conservatory are painted in a unifying off-white

updating a tired kitchen

46   **right** Gary and Melanie's kitchen is long overdue a facelift.

the problem

Gary Wilbourne and Melanie Taylor's flat in Bedhampton near Portsmouth with its dark wood units, copper cooker hood and worn-out flooring isn't going to appeal to anyone.

this room has plenty of light and with the new pale units, the walls can now take a splash of colour

above With white units, you can afford to be a bit brave with the wall colour.

the solution

The units are brightened up with a coat of neutral paint, a new floor is laid, and the copper cooker hood is removed and replaced with a useful shelf. This room has plenty of light and with the new pale units, the walls can now take a splash of colour. This breaks the golden rule that neutral colours work best, but where there are only small areas of wall, and there is a lot of natural light, a deep Victorian red, which is used here, can work well. There are times when it pays to know when to break the rules.

cost: £120

creating a dining space within the kitchen

right The huge American fridge dominates the Johnson's kitchen.

opposite The pine shelves and curtains complement the Aga.

the problem

Alan and Julie Johnson have a long narrow kitchen with plenty of room for a dining area but the room is too crowded with furniture and appliances. The kitchen is cluttered and the décor needs updating. It has been decorated in a rustic style with yellow brick pillars supporting open shelves. The room is dominated by a cosy blue Aga that has been placed in an alcove built in the same brick. There are several open pine shelves and a good quality dark slate floor. In spite of having big double patio doors opening onto the garden and another large window, the room feels oppressive.

the solution

When Alan and Julie first put their house on the market they did pack up a lot of their clutter and stored it in the garage. In order to make the kitchen look bigger, they have removed an old pine dresser and painted the walls white. But more needs to be done. The couple need to create a dining area at the end of the kitchen next to the patio doors. To make more room, the large American-style fridge-freezer is moved to the garage, and a pretty round plywood table with an easy wipe-clean formica top and four pale wood chairs are hired. There isn't time to box in the boiler, so a large plant in a fashionable raffia pot is used to disguise it.

Andrew says: If nowhere else, keep your kitchen spotless. Shining taps say 'clean house'.

the couple need to create a dining area at the end of the kitchen next to the patio doors

To take the edge off the country look and give the kitchen a more contemporary feel, the brick pillars and the brick alcove where the Aga sits are also painted white. The butler sink and Victorian-style brass taps stay.

Open shelves full of pots and pans look untidy. The cheapest way of hiding these is to curtain them off. Here the two open shelf units each side of the Aga are given curtains with simple but smart beige and grey stripes.

Clearing away almost all of Alan and Julie's remaining clutter completes the look. A pine plate rack, arranged with a few plates, stays. A large pine shelving unit is given the show house treatment. A collection of designer glass jars of varying sizes are filled with everyday items such as tea bags, coffee, flour, muesli and rice, and Julie's collection of Portuguese blue patterned ceramics are put on display.

51

opposite With the fridge moved to the garage, there's room for a table and chairs.

above Open shelves are a great way of displaying Julie's favourite crockery.

left Curtains are the quickest and easiest way to disguise untidy shelves.

Andrew says: Don't forget the rubbish – keep bins clean and fresh.

cost:
£470

to give the kitchen a more contemporary feel, the brick pillars and alcove where the Aga sits are painted white

putting a cooker into a kitchen

54

above Without a cooker, Gill's kitchen looks soulless and unused.

opposite The kitchen is given red accents in both the décor and the accessories.

the problem

Gill Davis's top-floor flat in Surbiton in Surrey has no cooker, which will make the flat difficult to sell because even people who microwave most of their food still expect to see a cooker in the kitchen.

the solution

Find room for a cooker and introduce a few stylish touches in an otherwise dull kitchen. This is potentially an attractive room. It is light and airy with a huge roof light with views over the Victorian rooftops. A smart new black gas cooker is bought and installed in the space by the fridge-freezer. This won't be a waste of Gill's money because the cooker is freestanding so she can take it with her when she moves. The kitchen cabinets are given a facelift with new pale wood doors and sleek stainless steel handles. The walls are given a coat of white paint. Gill owns a sweet ceramic chicken with a red daisy pattern, which provides the key for the red accent colour that is used to brighten the room.

cost:
£900

A row of hooks by the kitchen door is used to display a blue and red daisy-patterned tea cosy and oven gloves and two white and red tea towels. Above this a grey metal notice board has magnets decorated with a red flower pattern. Two wicker baskets on the washing machine are used as a laundry basket and for storage, and reveal an apron in the same blue and red daisy pattern as the tea cosy.

A new stainless steel shelf is erected on the wall above the fridge-freezer and is used to display some red glass tumblers, two red bowls and Gill's ceramic chicken. The red theme combined with brushed steel is continued on the work surface above the long run of units. On display are some shiny red storage jars, two red cups and saucers, a brushed steel bread bin, a cafétière and a toaster.

This kitchen now looks like a proper kitchen where food is prepared, and with a new dining area installed in the living room, there is even somewhere to eat it.

This kitchen now looks like a proper kitchen where food is prepared

the
dining room

the dining room

58

No home should be without a clearly defined dining room or dining area. Even busy professionals, who may not do much cooking, like the idea of entertaining their friends around a candle-lit table. And families who eat most of their meals on their knees in front of *EastEnders* still aspire to the ideal of large family gatherings in a spacious dining room or a dedicated eating area in a fashionable kitchen diner.

If you live in a house with a separate dining room that is rarely used, there is a temptation to make it double as an office or gym or a dumping ground for unwanted furniture that you can't bear to throw away. One of the golden rules of selling houses is to make sure that every room has a well-defined purpose. So a dining room should say dining room, and if there isn't anywhere else to put the computer or the gym equipment or the unwanted furniture, put it into storage.

The kitchen is often the hub of family life, which is why kitchens now double as dining rooms, but if you have a separate dining room, don't struggle to fit an eating area into your kitchen if it is too small. If yours is a kitchen diner, try and achieve a separate dining area with a table that isn't pushed against the wall.

Sometimes large living rooms have to double as dining rooms, especially in open-plan houses. Again create a dedicated dining space and think about installing a folding screen between the sitting and dining areas. In very small sitting rooms or kitchens that have to double as dining rooms look for clever foldaway tables and chairs that can be tucked away when not in use.

tips

A dining room can be a big plus. However, if the room is only used on special occasions, it can look gloomy and unloved. Make sure the room looks used by putting in fresh flowers and even think about laying the table for a formal dinner party, bringing out your best china and crystal glasses. Subtle lighting and candles can help create a feeling of sophistication.

Get the lighting right. Subtle low lighting in formal dining rooms works best. Install a light which pours pools of light over the table and fit a dimmer switch. In kitchen diners, which are used for family meals and smart dinner parties, lighting needs special attention. Avoid harsh strip lighting and install new halogen lights and dimmer switches.

Create a separate dining area in your kitchen. Kitchen diners are popular with families, and even if you have a separate dining room, it is worth creating an eating area in your kitchen if it is large enough.

Andrew says: Clean or replace stained carpets.

Narrow galley kitchens need a sense of space. *Narrow galley kitchens can also have a separate eating area but here it is best to avoid breakfast bars or extra L-shape units that divide the room up and make it look smaller.*

Where space is limited use small foldaway tables and chairs. Small foldaway tables and chairs that can be folded against the wall or hung on hooks are a good idea in small kitchens if there is nowhere else to eat.

Create a dining area in an underused space. *Take a close look at the spaces in your house. A clearly defined dining area can be created in a hall or living room. If the living room is full of furniture, lose some of it and replace it with a small dining table and chairs.*

Don't let the dining table become messy. Kitchen and dining tables are multi-purpose, so they can get filled with the children's homework, piles of unpaid bills and a trail of wires to the sewing machine or the laptop computer. Clear the clutter away and put out a big bowl of fresh fruit or a vase of bright flowers instead.

Think about repainting. *There is a fashion for painting dining rooms in strong colours such as terracotta and deep green. These colours can look very intimate and cosy at night but they are a minority taste and could well put off buyers. Think about repainting in a more neutral colour.*

Make a display. Dining rooms often have a glass-fronted cabinet or sideboard. Make the most of these by clearing out any junk and making attractive displays of the family dinner service and cut glass. Pretty candlesticks and decanters make attractive displays on the sideboard or mantelpiece. But put away that tray of half-finished bottles of whisky, gin and that foul-tasting aperitif you brought back from your last holiday in Spain. Kitchen tables that have seen better days can be disguised under a tablecloth and enlivened with a large bowl of fresh fruit.

Large kitchens can be separated into two distinct sections. *One section can be dedicated to cooking, the other for dining. Do this by dividing the two areas with a breakfast bar, which provides extra eating space for quick meals and snacks.*

Keep a separate dining room. Don't be tempted to convert a separate dining room and living room into one large room. This won't help you sell the house – many people want a separate dining room, and those that don't will be able to do the conversion for themselves relatively cheaply.

Andrew says: Good lighting is essential for atmosphere. Avoid fluorescent and economy lightbulbs as these create yellow, gloomy light.

modernise a dated dining room

below Gay and Keith in their new-look dining room.

opposite The hired furniture adds to the unified look of the downstairs rooms.

the problem

The Keavenys' modern house in Croydon looks old-fashioned and needs to be brought up-to-date. The downstairs rooms are all linked and need to have a modern, unified look. The couple have already laid a smart wood laminate floor in the kitchen, but the hall, dining room and sitting room are decorated in clashing styles that went out of fashion fifteen years ago. One wall of the dining room is covered in large school photographs in their ugly brown mounts, which won't be of any interest to potential buyers. The pale blue wallpaper and floral border are dated and the dark wooden furniture is oppressive.

the solution

Link the dining room stylistically to the rest of the downstairs rooms and update the décor and furnishings. The pale blue carpet is just two months old, but it has to go. It is put into storage along with the dining room table and chairs, and the messy bookshelves, CDs, videos and books. A wood laminate floor is laid that matches the one in the kitchen. The family portraits are removed and the wallpaper is stripped

the room now looks clean and modern

and repainted in a neutral shade. The room now looks clean and modern. What it still needs, however, is modern furniture. If your furniture isn't up to scratch, think about hiring furniture from a specialist firm for the time that it takes you to sell your house. The Keavenys agree to hire a modern pale wood table and four Arne Jacobson chairs. The look is completed with a new minimalist lamp, pale linen curtains and a large glass vase filled with glamorous lilies.

cost:
£290

turn a child's bedroom into a dining room

above The original fireplace – an important selling feature – can hardly be seen.

opposite Back to its roots, the back room becomes a place to eat once more.

the problem

Coco and Tak's house has two reception rooms. The one at the front of the house is a spacious sitting room, but the one at the back, which should be a dining room, has been turned into a child's bedroom. To meet buyers' expectations, it must be returned to its original use.

the solution

The bunk beds and children's clutter are removed. The old-fashioned carpet is lifted and a wood laminate floor is laid, helping to define the area as a light, practical dining space. Period features such as fireplaces are a big selling point in Victorian houses, but the fireplace in this room needs sprucing up to remove old paint splashes and layers of grime. The walls are painted a neutral shade to match the newly painted hall and landing. The table and chairs are moved from the kitchen. Coco has some lovely old millinery blocks that she arranges artistically on the mantelpiece.

cost: **£135**

Period features such as fireplaces are a big selling point in Victorian houses

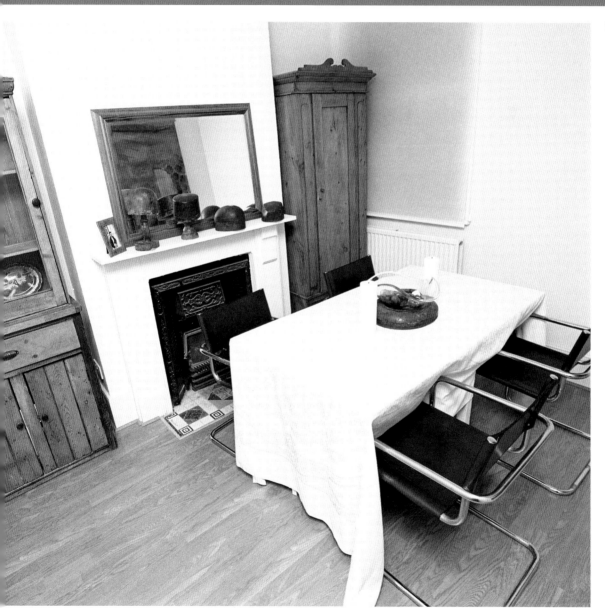

rearrange the living rooms to create a separate dining room

right The Johnsons' narrow sitting room would be much better suited to a dining area.

the problem

Alan and Julie Johnson's house has two separate living rooms, one at the front of the house and one at the back with double patio doors overlooking a terrace and the garden. At the moment, the family use the room at the back as their sitting room. The front room has an unusual oak-panelled bar and a baby grand piano, both of which take up a great deal of space. The bar originally came in handy because they used to throw a lot of parties. Now the room is hardly used, except as a passageway through to the living room and kitchen. Two arches of decorative red brick separate the two rooms.

The back room, which is being used as a living room, is long and narrow. The swirly carpet and heavy fireplace surround look very old-fashioned, and the end of the room is dead unused space, except for a built-in bookcase. A major transformation is required.

the solution

Rearrange the rooms by turning the front room into a chic modern living room, and creating a dining room in the back room with a separate reading area in the unused space by the patio doors. Alan and Julie have already filled up their garage with boxes full of clutter, so the larger items have to go into storage. Out goes the couple's furniture; in comes a vanload of hired furniture to give the rooms that show house look.

Pulling up the carpet reveals the original wood parquet flooring. The couple kept the floor covered with carpet and expected to find that it was damaged. In fact the floor was in almost perfect condition. The room, including the dado rail and the red brick arches, are all painted in a neutral shade of beige. There isn't time to rip out the old-fashioned stone fireplace. Instead the dark leatherette seats each side of the fireplace are replaced with simple painted wooden seats and blue cushions, and the dark mantelpiece and low

shelf are painted in the same neutral colour.

The hired table is pale wood with stainless steel legs; the chairs have padded seats and backs upholstered in dark blue brushed cotton. A matching pale wood sideboard gives this new dining room a clean, sophisticated look.

A cosy reading area is created at the end of the room. The bookshelves are cleared and painted, a brown leather chair is installed together with a stainless-steel reading light. The two areas, the dining space and reading area, each have a pale coir rug to reinforce the idea that this room now has two separate functions.

Neutral colours and modern furniture on their own can look bleak and uninviting. This is where the clever use of accessories comes into its own. In Alan and Julie's dining room, accessories are used to maximum effect. The colour scheme in the room is basically blue and cream and these colours are picked up in the accessories with a few additional splashes of colour. On the sideboard there are two tall blue glass vases, another

above By hiring a dining table that suits the shape of the room, this space feels less like a corridor.

the dark leatherette seats each side of the fireplace are replaced with simple painted wooden seats and blue cushions

below The shelves and chair makes this a quiet reading corner.

opposite A bright display of red berries and a modern-art print finish the room's contemporary look.

smaller one in turquoise and an unusual large hexagonal red candle, all arranged in a little cluster. Two shiny stainless steel vases filled with decorative red berry twigs stand on the table. Another stainless steel vase, along with two tall dark blue pillar candles, decorate the mantelpiece. A neatly stacked pile of logs, a large blue vase filled with tall willow twigs, a large red glass vase

and two pictures simply propped against the wall all make strong statements on the long low shelf. They are smart contemporary features and act to counterbalance the dated stone wall. To further break up the wall, a floating shelf with two dark bamboo containers is erected high on the wall at the end of the room by the patio doors.

The shelves in the reading corner, which extend over the arch into the kitchen, have been in the house ever since Alan and Julie moved in. Once they are painted the same neutral colour as the rest of the room and cleared of their clutter, they emerge as a modern feature, with shelves of differing heights and cubbyholes for displays. Here you find the couple's CD collection, displays of magazines, travel books with decorative covers, candles and rows of little tea lights in blue glass containers. The shelves are now transformed into an interesting feature in their own right. And to complete the look pale linen curtains are hung on a stainless steel rails replacing the old heavy blue curtains on their dark mahogany pole.

cost:
£584
including £90 for furniture hire (per month)

injecting some style into a dull dining room

right The fussy curtains dominate Mark and Miriam's dining room.

opposite Clean lines and plenty of light make the room worthy of any show home.

the problem

Mark and Miriam Krepka's modern house in Bedfordshire is only five years old but it looks dated. The dining room is the first room that greets you as you enter the house, so it needs to pack a visual punch. At the moment the room is just dull. There is a round table with four clumpy upholstered chairs and the room is dominated by the old-fashioned flower pattern net curtains and drab curtains with patterned borders and tie backs. The room is painted yellow, which clashes with the deep raspberry colour carpet. The room looks as if it belongs to someone several generations older than Mark and Miriam.

the solution

Create a good-looking, contemporary dining room that will appeal to buyers as soon as they cross the threshold. Mark and Miriam's house is up against the many new houses that are being built in the town, so to compete, it must look like a show house. The raspberry colour carpet runs throughout the house and Mark and Miriam can't afford to change it. Instead, the colour schemes for the house must work with it. The hall is painted a fairly strong shade of green, which goes well with the pink of the carpet, so it is decided to adopt tones of green and beige as the unifying theme for the ground floor.

cost:
£155
including £90 for furniture hire (per month)

a new oval table and four chairs with beige linen seats are hired

The existing table and chairs go into storage and a new oval table and four chairs with beige linen seats are hired. The room is painted a calming shade of sage green. Here the main decorating motif is a pretty green and red chintz, which picks up on the overall green and pink theme. Three simple white roman blinds with small panels of chintz at the bottom are fitted to the windows overlooking the garden. The table is decorated with a red runner with a central panel of the same chintz. A tall fluted glass vase filled with white lilies completes the effect.

The glass-panelled doors between the hall and the dining room are left open to give the house a feeling of spaciousness. This once dowdy dining room has now been transformed into a light and airy room that creates a good impression and sets the tone for the rest of the house.

the
sitting room

chapter
six

the sitting room

The sitting room is the one room in the house that is dedicated entirely to leisure and it should be both relaxing and elegant. Your buyers must be able to imagine themselves unwinding there at the end of the day and impressing their friends with their impeccable taste.

A sitting room benefits from a focal point and in many period houses this is provided by the fireplace. A working fireplace with a real, roaring log fire is a big selling point in a country property, but an imitation coal-effect gas fire is often what buyers prefer in smaller town houses. If the fireplace doesn't have some sort of fire, decorate it with an imaginative display (see below).

Smart modern furniture upholstered in plain neutral fabrics works best, but don't despair if your furniture is at the end of its life because there are plenty of low-cost tricks of the trade that you can use to disguise it.

tips

Rearrange your mantelpiece. Take a critical look at the clutter on your mantelpiece. Remove most of it and make a display of a few choice objects, such as candlesticks complete with tall elegant candles, a collection of colour-coordinated vases, or a row of three identical vases arranged in a row, each with one simple bloom.

Give the room a heart. Creating a focal point for your sitting room will give it a welcoming feel. If there is an existing fireplace, make sure it is restored, and if it is working, get the chimney swept. Remove old-fashioned granny-style gas fires, and replace with a coal-effect fire in a traditional grate. If the fireplace has been blocked up, make a simple, low-cost fireplace by unblocking it, erecting a simple shelf on the wall above, and inserting a grate into the opened-up space. Non-functioning fireplaces can be dressed with a pile of logs, a cluster of giant pine cones, or a pretty display of fairy lights.

Disguise old sofas and chairs. If your sofas and chairs look tired and grubby, cover them with an inexpensive throw in neutral colours and invest in some cushions to give the room a dash of colour. Alternatively, you could have your sofas and chairs recovered or you could put them into storage and hire modern ones.

Arrange the furniture carefully. The traditional lounge suite of a sofa and two chairs can make a room look busy and unstructured. Two sofas work better, so think about putting the chairs into storage and buying a small sofa from a chain store or hiring one. Arrange the furniture around a low table for a more coherent look.

Make sure the television doesn't dominate. It's a fact of life: most people watch TV in their living rooms and with televisions getting bigger and more sophisticated, it is easy for it to dominate the room. It isn't necessary to hide the television, but make sure it doesn't look as if it is the only activity that goes on in the room.

Pay attention to the flooring. Living room carpets get a lot of heavy wear. There may be worn patches in front of the sofas and chairs, and stains such as red wine that can be difficult to remove. Shampoo the carpets or get them cleaned professionally – probably cheaper than you think. If there is a lovely parquet floor lurking beneath your carpet, take up the carpet and flaunt it. And if the carpet is really past it, throw it out, and sand or paint the floorboards. Rugs and floorboards are always a better bet than an old moth-eaten carpet.

Think about the curtains. Thick, dark curtains are often used in living rooms to give the room a cosy, warm feeling on winter evenings. But they can also make a room appear small and poky, especially if you are trying to sell it in summer. Simple light-coloured curtains or roman blinds open up a room and will work better while you are selling.

Consider the lighting. Lighting is vital in the sitting room. You need to have a variety of different sources of light. These will include a central pendant and wall lights equipped with simple neutral lamp shades, table lamps and perhaps one directional light, such as a standard lamp for reading by. When showing a sitting room in the evenings, use the table lamps, which cast the room in a soft glow, and place a book or some needlework under the reading light to give the impression of quiet, contemplative activity.

Create a dining area. If there is no separate dining room and there is no room in the kitchen either, you will have to create a well-defined dining area in the sitting room. To make room you may have to dispose or store some of your sitting room furniture, but it will pay dividends because a house without a separate dining area is difficult to sell.

Andrew says: Make sure your home is a comfortable temperature. Buyers don't want to break into a sweat!

making the most of period features

right Ann's living room appears dark and cluttered.

opposite A country cottage for contemporary living.

the problem

Ann Stolworthy has used strong colours throughout her seventeenth-century cottage in north Staffordshire. In her living room, which is open to the ceiling rafters, the walls and ceiling have been rag rolled terracotta and there is a pattern of trailing leaves over part of the ceiling. Heavy blue curtains hang over the French windows leading to the garden, and the walls are hung with pictures in ornate frames. This is not a fashionable look, and it doesn't show the room's lovely wooden beams to their best advantage.

the solution

Throughout the cottage, many of Ann's strong colours have been replaced with crisp white paint, including the sitting room. Far from being a strange idea, it makes the rooms look bigger and emphasises the beauty of the mellow wood beams without detracting from the cottage feel.

There is a tendency to fill cottages up with lots of clutter, but this can make the rooms look small and poky. The aim here is to open up the sitting room and make it feel more spacious. The dark blue curtains are taken down and the windows are left unadorned, revealing a view of the garden. Most of the pictures are taken down and stored.

The wood burning stove, which provides the room with its focal point, is given a new lease of life with a coat of good old-fashioned blacking. Two huge white throws disguise the slightly saggy sofas. The red and white theme that is seen throughout the house is continued with a scatter of red and white cushions.

The leafy mural on the sitting room ceiling, which must have taken many hours to paint, is erased with a coat of white paint. That took courage, but Ann admits that her new white sitting room is a vast improvement on what was there before.

cost: £130

the aim is to open up the room and make it feel more spacious

making a bleak loft-style room look chic

78

the problem

Alicia McDonnell's loft-style Manchester flat should appeal to aspirational young professional buyers, but the main living area lacks any sense of inner-city chic. There is a vast expanse of bare red brick wall. The room has high ceilings but the bare concrete beams look like a city car park rather than a smart urban pad. The full-length windows are an attractive feature but the view is bleak and there is no privacy at night.

The flat has been rented out and Alicia hasn't paid any attention to the furniture. It is furnished with bits and bobs. The old-fashioned leather sofa and armchair with their dated patterned cushions could have come from Alicia's granny's house. The dining table and four fold-up metal chairs are dull to the point of boredom. The coffee table jammed up against the unadorned full length window and the lonely standard lamp conspire to make the room look unloved and austere.

the solution

Alicia needs to give this room the cool modern look that will appeal to young professional buyers. As Andrew Winter says, it needs to become 'a desirable designer pad with attitude'. Alicia must create a feeling of space while at the same time dividing up the room into different areas, creating somewhere to sit and relax and somewhere to eat.

Her first step must be to jettison all her furniture and hire a room full of new furnishings. Furniture hire is a growing business. Hired furniture is used by house builders in their show homes, but an increasing number of ordinary house sellers find it is a cheap way of giving their home a face-lift. Alicia's new furniture would have cost her £7,000 to buy. Hiring it costs her £570 a month, but hopefully she will get the money back when she sells her flat for a better price.

Alicia ropes in her friends for a painting party. With ladders and long-handled paint rollers they get to work painting the room white. Out goes the dull grey concrete ceiling, which is now a sparkling white, making the whole room look lighter and brighter.

The red brick wall stays as this is what buyers expect in a loft-style development, but it is a large expanse and needs to be broken up. A big abstract picture would be the obvious solution but Alicia's budget doesn't stretch that far. Instead, four square canvas panels are painted in shades of blue, turquoise and bright fuchsia pink and these are hung on the wall in a square pattern to provide instant colour and interest. An additional splash of colour is added to the alcove, which is painted in the same shade of turquoise as the kitchen. Alicia hangs a fashionable wall-mounted CD player here.

The room is crying out for contemporary furniture, and Alicia has chosen to hire two cream sofas in a modern boxy style. The look is softened with cushions in cream, black and turquoise to match the painted panels, the alcove and kitchen. Creating the illusion of space is important in a loft-style flat like this so a round glass dining table is hired, around which are placed four modern leather-seated chairs.

The idea that the room has two separate areas is emphasised with the use of matching rugs, one under the coffee table by the sofa, the other under the dining table. And to complement the chic, modern look, there is a large vase of arum lilies on the dining table, and arrangements of small ornaments that pick up on the turquoise

Alicia's new furniture would have cost her £7,000 to buy

and blue theme. Privacy is achieved without sacrificing the lightness of the room by hanging simple white blinds.

Before, it was hard to see who might want to live in this dark and dingy room. Now, by the simple expedient of filling it with just a few pieces of modern furniture, young professionals won't have any difficulty imagining their lives unfold in this space.

80   **right** A glass dining table fits unobtrusively into the room.

opposite
Neutrals with bold accents bring the room into the twenty-first century.

Andrew says: Don't think the furniture in your house doesn't affect its sales value – it does. Bad furniture says you don't care about the house, while good furniture says you do.

cost:
£750
including £570 for
furniture hire (per month)

giving a drab sitting room that 'show house' look

below Mark and Miriam's suite appears dated and dark.

opposite The new arrangement makes the fireplace, rather than the television, the focus of the sitting room.

the problem

Mark and Miriam's sitting room in their modern house in Sandy in Bedfordshire is a lovely big room but the decoration is unattractive and the room looks dark, cramped and dull. The walls are painted red and clash with the raspberry carpet. The sofa and two chairs are leather and tartan and lack style. And to make matters worse, they are arranged in a line facing a giant television that dominates the room. There are double patio doors leading to the garden, but these are obscured by fussy full-length net curtains.

the solution

Import some style, so the house can compete with all the brand-new houses nearby. Starting from scratch, the room is emptied of all its furniture, which is put into storage. The aim is to make the room feel bigger, lighter and airier and to link it stylistically to the other downstairs rooms. Out go the net curtains and the heavy cream curtains with their plaited tiebacks.

Even though it is only five years old, the carpet has faded badly and as a completely different layout is being planned, a new carpet is essential. A colour scheme of greens and beiges has been planned around the carpet in the rest of the downstairs rooms, so the sitting room gets a new carpet in the same raspberry colour.

The walls are painted a pale shade of green with fresh white woodwork. Green is a calm, restful colour and immediately the room seems larger. New furniture is hired and arranged to give the room a more intimate feel. Two classic cream sofas with feet and brass casters are arranged opposite each other around a pale wood coffee table. The room is large enough for the sofas to stand away from the walls, which gives the impression of lots of easy circulation space.

The sofas are at right angles to the pretty Adam-style fireplace with its beige marble fascia and hearth. The fireplace now becomes the focus of the room rather than the television, which is tidily tucked away on a table in the corner by the patio doors.

the finished room is simple and elegant, and all evidence of the children has been erased

90 **below** Decorated with silk cushions, the Coleman's sofa is given the prominence it deserves.

a feeling of opulence. The modern sofa is partly covered with a burgundy fleece throw. The hard square lines of the sofa are softened with two pillow size cream damask cushions that provide a link with the damask sofa, and a square cream silk cushion. The damask sofa has two burgundy silk cushions with damask panels and silk tassels at each corner and two cream silk cushions.

Touches of chintz are used throughout the house. A clever idea for pictures is to take samples of chintz patterned wallpaper, put them in cream mounts and place them in pretty painted frames. These chintz pictures feature in several

places in the Colemans' house. Here a red chintz picture hanging behind the damask sofa finds an echo in the cushion cover on the wicker chair.

Placing a mirror above the mantelpiece is a traditional trick for making a sitting room look bigger. A large mirror can be placed centrally over the mantelpiece, but here a smaller mirror with a chunky gold surround is placed asymmetrically and balanced with a small picture of a field full

of red poppies. The mantelpiece itself is decorated with some elegant candles which, when lit,
add to the ambient lighting provided by the small
brass lamp in the corner of the room.

The finished room is now simple and elegant,
and all evidence of the children has been erased
with the exception of a small wicker basket of
children's books and two small silver-framed photographs on the shelf next to the television.

cost:
£513

left A room for
grown-ups.

adding a dining area to a sitting room

below Gill's sitting room is full of personal touches that will prevent buyers seeing themselves living in the flat.

the problem

The living room in Gill Davis's top-floor flat is cluttered and old-fashioned and there is nowhere in the flat to eat. There is a heavy carved bookshelf packed with paperbacks Gill may never read again. A mirror with an ornate carved frame and a small sculpture sit on the top. One of the walls has a jumbled display of paintings, a plate and various knick-knacks. The sofa and chairs are upholstered in a shiny, striped damask material, which simply adds to the confusion of the room.

two small two-seater sofas take up less space than a traditional three-piece suite

the solution

Give the room a fresh new look and a dining area by putting most of the furniture into storage and hiring two new sofas and a dining table and chairs. The magnolia paint is replaced with white and the two small triangles of terracotta paint in the window recesses are painted cream.

Two small two-seater sofas take up less space than a traditional three-piece suite, freeing up space for a dining table. The colour scheme chosen for this room – camel, brown and maroon with splashes of orange – is cool and sophisticated.

One of the camel-coloured sofas is placed under the dormer window, the other at right angles to it, providing a relaxed and sociable space for entertaining friends. Gill's chunky dark wood Indian coffee table is used to display some carefully chosen ornaments to good effect. Two small brown suede cubes on the other side of the

table provide extra seating without taking up too much space.

Colour and texture is added to the sofas with cushions and throws, some in maroon, others in shaggy brown Mongolian lamb. A dark brown chenille throw is draped over the arm of one sofa; the other gets a throw of bright orange mohair. A little pine table has been hired and placed in the corner to house Gill's music centre and CD collection. On top, a silver-based table lamp with a brown shade will give subtle light for evening viewings.

A round pale wood table and two dining chairs with maroon upholstered seats and backs are hired to create a separate dining area close to the kitchen. Before, it was unclear how anyone cooked or ate in this flat because there was neither a cooker in the kitchen nor a dining table in the living room. Now potential buyers won't be put off by the lack of these basic facilities.

above By rearranging the furniture, room is made for a small dining table.

left Two small sofas take up less space than a three-piece suite.

cost:
£350
including £180 for
furniture hire (per month)

chapter
seven

the
bathroom

the bathroom

96

A really swish kitchen or bathroom can clinch a deal because buyers can forgive almost anything if the kitchens and bathrooms don't need ripping out as soon as they move in. A large bathroom, with a bath, basin, toilet and separate shower will help sell your house, but even small bathrooms can make a big impression if they are kept looking clean, bright and airy.

Bathrooms get a lot of heavy use and can end up looking grimy and smelling damp if they aren't given a facelift every couple of years, so before you do anything else get busy with the scrubbing brush and bleach.

Bathroom design has undergone a quiet revolution over the last few years. Mosaic, marble and limestone are replacing tiles; baths double as showers; toilets have their cisterns hidden behind the wall; basins have been redesigned as bowls that sit on wooden or glass shelves. The biggest status symbol of all is a wet room, with a shower that drains directly into the floor. And there is still the enduring fashion for the Victorian-style bathroom, which has as its centrepiece a freestanding claw-foot bath with a traditional brass mixer tap and shower attachment.

Andrew says: Toilets should *always* be clean with the seat down.

These may be the bathrooms to which we all aspire but that doesn't mean you have to spend mega bucks to create a bathroom that sells your house. Take a critical look at your bathroom. It will probably take less than a weekend's work to transform even the direst bathroom into a space where your buyers can imagine having a long soak in a relaxing bath perfumed with scented bath oils.

tips

Bathrooms must be spotlessly clean and shiny. Scrub every inch of your bathroom, removing limescale from round the taps, cleaning around the bath seal and sealing again if necessary. If the grouting between the tiles looks grubby, regrout with a grouting pen. Polish mirrors and taps to a high shine.

White bathroom suites work best. Coloured bathroom suites should be replaced if they are looking tired. A basic bath, hand basin and toilet from a builders' merchant or DIY store costs less than you think – around £300.

Renew the tiles rather than the bathroom suite. If you have a coloured suite that is still in good condition, it may be the matching coloured tiles that are making your bathroom look dated. Instead of replacing the suite, think about replacing the tiles with plan white ones which can in many cases be simply fixed on top of the old tiles.

Replace the radiator with a heated towel rail. *A smart chrome, heated towel rail means an end to soggy towels and makes a big impression with buyers.*

Re-enamel a stained bath. Cast-iron baths are expensive but popular. Instead of ripping out the whole bath and putting in a cheaper alternative get the enamel replaced. The Yellow Pages lists the names of local firms who can do this.

Add a shower attachment to the bath. *For busy families and younger buyers, a shower is a big selling point – the more powerful the better.*

Replace the shower curtain. Shower curtains need replacing frequently, so get a new one before your first buyer arrives. Avoid novelty designs which have limited appeal. Play safe with a plain design and make sure your rail is secure. Or better still, think of installing a simple glass shower panel at the side of the bath instead.

Invest in some white fluffy towels. *A pile of white fluffy towels and a good quality bath mat add a glamorous touch.*

Clear away the clutter and make a display of a few top-of-the-range toiletries. No one wants to see budget bottles of shampoo, saggy old toothbrushes or half-squeezed tubes of toothpaste, so tidy them away somewhere. Put out a fresh bar of soap and have fun buying two or three bottles of the prettiest toiletries for display.

Andrew says: *Be critical of your home.* If a house like yours has been sold but it had a new bathroom and yours doesn't, don't expect yours to sell for the same price.

Replace the bath panel. *It is easy to forget the bath panel, but if yours is looking worn or old-fashioned, replacing it is a simple task. Baths come in standard sizes so finding a new panel to fit isn't difficult. Builders' merchants and do-it-yourself stores offer a good choice of panels in plastic or wood. Or you might strike lucky and find a claw-foot bath behind the bath panel, in which case make this a feature by painting the outside of the bath and running the flooring under the bath.*

Tongue-and-groove panelling is a timeless look. Look-alike painted tongue-and-groove panelling that can now be bought in sheets. This can transform a tired bathroom at minimal expense. Line the walls up to hip height, and top with a small shelf that can be used for displays.

Rip up the carpet. *Carpets don't work in bathrooms. They get wet, look tatty and can smell. Replace it with vinyl or cork which are easy to clean, or paint the floorboards after sealing the gaps between the boards.*

adding a toilet to a bathroom

the solution

A new white three-piece bathroom suite is fitted in order to make room for a toilet. A simple bathroom suite is not difficult to install if you use the services of a qualified plumber, but remember it is important to measure the room carefully before ordering to make sure it fits. Here, the bath is moved from under the window to along the longer wall, and the toilet is fitted next to it. The old carpet is removed and the floor is checked for protruding nails before laying a new black and white vinyl floor. The bathroom is at last fit for a family.

Andrew says: No matter what their style and size, bathrooms must say *clean*, *relaxing* and *functional*.

above Even without a toilet, the Blakes' bathroom is crowded.

opposite A smaller bath and basin make room for a toilet.

the problem

Alison and Sean Blake's ex-council house doesn't have a toilet in the bathroom. This makes the house unattractive to families with small children, who are their most likely buyers. The idea of having to traipse downstairs in the middle of the night to take small children to the toilet is an unappealing prospect.

cost:
£590

replacing a worn-out bathroom

opposite These days most buyers will be looking for a white bathroom suite like Ann's new one.

the problem

Ann Stolworthy's bathroom needs a total facelift. The beige bathroom suite looks dowdy, the tiles are cracked, the grouting dirty and there is mould round the bath. There are some lifeless grey stripy curtains, and the walls above the tiles are painted pink. Ann knows the bathroom is putting off buyers but she is reluctant to spend the money if she is moving.

the bathroom is now as fresh and clean-looking as the rest of the house

cost:
£360

the solution

Ann is persuaded that changing her bathroom is essential and that it won't cost her a fortune. The old beige bath, basin and toilet are replaced with a simple, basic white suite. By shopping around and comparing prices at local builders' merchants, plumbers' merchants and do-it-yourself stores, Ann found she could replace her bathroom suite for around £300, which is a very small outlay if it helps to sell her house.

The worn cork tiles are pulled up to reveal the original oak floorboards. There isn't time to sand them so instead the gaps between the floorboards are sealed and the boards are painted with a white waterproof paint usually reserved for boats. The pink walls are painted white, a simple pine bath panel is added and a new white framed mirror with its own little shelf is hung on the wall.

The colour scheme in Ann's cottage is now predominantly white but with splashes of red. In the bathroom, a bar of dark pink soap rests on a pretty red floral soap dish, and bottles of toiletries and lavender water with white and red labels are grouped on the shelf. The bathroom is now as fresh and clean-looking as the rest of the house. Before it was letting the house down; now buyers will no longer see it as a potential expense.

the
bedroom

the bedroom

A good bedroom will feel like a quiet sanctuary, a place where buyers can imagine unwinding at the end of the day, kicking off their shoes for a quick snooze before heading for the bright lights on a Saturday night, or indulging in a leisurely breakfast in bed with the Sunday newspapers.

Understated colours such as lilac, pale blue, and pale green are restful and relaxing and can be used instead of neutral shades to bring a touch of romance and glamour to the bedroom.

The main bedroom is frequently one of the biggest, lightest and airiest rooms in the house, so it is always worth thinking about how to show it to its best advantage. In Victorian terrace houses, for example, it is often the large room at the front on the first floor. In this very common house type, it is likely to be the only room that spans the entire width of the house and could well have a lovely bow window and another window – attractive features for potential buyers.

Achieving a comfortable and relaxed feel is the first priority when giving a bedroom buyer appeal. ...ed should be the focal point. Make sure its ...ered with a bedspread or a simple ...igh with pretty colour coordi-...ns. After the bed, the ...ned, built-in cup-...gh any wardrobes ...f life with a neutral

tips

Double beds are best. If there is enough room, put in a double bed, even if it is only a small one. You can then advertise it as a double bedroom in the estate agent's particulars.

Place the bed carefully. Don't put the long side of a bed against a wall. This gives the impression of a bed that is difficult to make. Place it so there is access from three sides. If there is a good view from the window, place the bed facing the window.

Bedside tables are essential. Everything you need in bed must be close at hand, so buyers will expect to see a bedside table each side of a double bed and on one side of a single bed. Make sure it is tidy: an alarm clock, a lamp for reading, the latest Booker prize-winning novel, and one or two treasured possessions artfully arranged, is all you need.

Provide lights to read by. For many people reading in bed is one of life's greatest pleasures. Make sure there are reading lights whose switches can be operated from bed. There is nothing more irritating than having to get out of bed to turn off the bedroom light – and buyers may well notice these small details.

Pay attention to storage. Roomy, well-designed, built-in storage with well-planned interiors complete with drawers, hanging space and room for shoes and bags is a big selling point. Think about clearing out your cupboards too. Buyers aren't always shy about opening cupboards and having a poke around. A well-ordered cupboard will give the impression that you are an organised person who has looked after the house.

Don't ignore the space under the bed. *Bedrooms are often short of storage, but the space under beds is frequently ignored. Contemporary wooden beds often come with matching wood drawers underneath. Plastic storage containers are a useful alternative: the ones with wheels are particularly handy. They are cheap and available from all the big chain stores and do-it-yourself stores, and worth investing in as they provide a useful hiding-place for clutter when viewers come to see your house, as well as giving an impression of a well-organised bedroom.*

Painted floorboards are fashionable. If your bedroom carpet is looking tatty and there are floorboards underneath, a cheap solution is to discard the carpet and paint the floorboards white or pale grey. This is likely to appeal to younger buyers, whereas replacing the carpet may be a better solution if your buyers are likely to be older.

Avoid bright bedlinen. Brightly coloured, patterned or novelty linen won't appeal to everyone.

White bedlinen works best. You can't go wrong with plain white bedlinen in pristine condition. It gives off a clean, fresh image. Alternatively, disguise your taste in bedlinen with a plain white or beige bedspread and invest in a few luxurious velvet and silk cushions for a touch of glamour.

Remove hooks on the door. All clothes should be put away. By removing any hooks you won't be tempted to hang clothes outside the cupboard.

Think about removing the dressing table. Dressing tables can look fussy and old-fashioned. Consider putting it into storage if this makes your bedroom look bigger and more contemporary.

Take care of original features. In older houses, bedrooms often have pretty cast-iron grates. Make these a feature of the room by cleaning them and placing a collection of church candles in them, or an arrangement of aromatic logs.

Andrew says: Ventilate bedrooms before viewing, but don't lose all the heat as they need to feel comfortable.

children's bedrooms

Children's rooms present a special problem when you are trying to sell your home. Children are great hoarders and they don't have a very well-developed sense of order. Teenagers, meanwhile, often express themselves with weird and wonderful colour schemes in their bedrooms. Negotiating the changes needed to sell the house requires tact and forward planning. And remember, if moving house is giving you panic attacks or tension headaches, it is likely to be equally stressful for your children.

In a family house, buyers expect to find children's rooms. They will make allowances for a certain amount of children's mess, but rooms that have been decorated to suit the needs of a particular child can be off-putting. For example, a bedroom done out with pink frills for a five-year-old daughter will not go down well with buyers with young sons who will only see a room that needs redecorating.

Andrew says: Make sure beds are made and there are no dirty socks on the floor.

tips

Ask your children to do a clear out. This has to be done before you move, so why delay? Do it now before the viewings start. Children often hate throwing their stuff away, so try the incentive of a car boot sale. Kids love the thrill of earning money from selling their old toys, books and games.

Buy plenty of matching storage boxes. You have probably got used to seeing piles of toys, books, games and craft materials strewn about the place, but it won't impress your buyers. All the chain stores now sell attractive storage boxes and they needn't cost a fortune. They come in a variety of different styles, but stick to one design and slide them neatly under the bed or make an attractive stack. Label them, so your children can find what they need quickly, and encourage them to tidy up when potential buyers are due.

Tackle the grime. Children's rooms take quite a battering. If the carpet has seen too many spills, shampoo it or get it professionally cleaned. If it is past rescuing, take it up and paint the floorboards with a hard-wearing floor paint and put down a rug. Even if the room doesn't need redecorating, the paint work may be chipped and scratched, in which case it is worth rubbing it down and repainting with fresh white gloss or eggshell paint.

Hide the novelty bedlinen. Your daughter's Barbie duvet cover won't go down well if your viewer happens to have a teenage son. If your son supports Manchester United, his treasured Beckham duvet cover might alienate your viewers if they support Arsenal. Plain bedlinen in a strong colour works best, or cover the offending duvet under a plain bedspread.

Cut down the number of posters and remove the stickers. Many children's rooms are plastered with posters, and mirrors and windows get covered in stickers. Remove stickers with hot soapy water and a paint scraper. Buy a big cardboard tube so your children can roll up and save the posters they want to take with them. Put a few of their favourites back on the wall in inexpensive clip frames.

Tackle experimental teenage décor. You may need every ounce of tact to persuade your wildly experimental teenager that their gothic temple of a bedroom could well scupper a sale. Reassure them that you are impressed by their creativity and that they will have a free rein in their new room.

Strong colours can work well. Children's rooms are best decorated in a simple, basic style which will suit children of either sex and any age at least initially. In most rooms neutral or pale colours work best, but in children's rooms, strong bright colours work equally well.

Andrew says: As long as the beds are made and the room is tidy children's rooms don't have to be off-putting. They can even be an advantage if your buyers have kids themselves.

Children's rooms are multi-purpose. Children's room are not just bedrooms, they are also the child's sanctuary. It is where they entertain their friends, do their homework, listen to music, or play on their computer. Their rooms need to be planned around a number of different activities. As well the bed and plenty of storage, a desk, good lighting and some comfy seating, such as a couple of brightly coloured bean bags, transform what could be just a boring bedroom into an attractive children's den.

Find somewhere to hide the hamster or gerbil. Small animals in cages make great children's pets but don't expect your viewers to be equally enthusiastic. Some people have an aversion to small rodents and unless their cages are regularly cleaned out they can smell. Hide these pets when buyers come around. Think about putting them in the garage or garden shed and give the room a good airing.

turning a workroom into a bedroom

right Who would guess this is the largest bedroom in the house?

opposite A tranquil haven where Coco and Tak can relax at the end of the day.

the solution

This room is transformed into a restful, glamorous bedroom with instant buyer appeal. Coco and Tak are sleeping in the smaller double bedroom where they opted for the hippy look, with a mattress on the floor and, strange for south-east London, a mosquito net! What Coco and Tak need is a proper grown-up bedroom in the large double room at the front of the house. This means putting their businesses on hold while they sell their house. Everything in the workshop is shipped off and put into storage while the dream bedroom is created. The walls are painted a restful shade of lilac, one of the best colours for a relaxing bedroom. A smart modern metal bed is installed, the first bed this room has seen in nine years. The floorboards are painted white, which reflects the light and covers up the less than perfect floorboards. The couple are keen collectors of modern art and a large colourful painting is placed behind the bed, with the vivid yellow colour picked up in the bedspread and cushions.

the problem

Coco and Tak Peppas live in a lovely three-bedroom Victorian terrace house in south-east London. The best room is the main bedroom on the first floor at the front of the house, which, with two big sash windows, is the biggest and brightest room in the house. The problem is the Peppas are using it as a workroom for Coco's millinery business and as a studio for the couple's design business. It is a mess and buyers fail to see the room's potential. It needs to be converted back into a bedroom.

everything in the workshop is shipped off and put into storage

cost:
£375

modernising a dated main bedroom

right and below
The built-in wardrobes dominate Alan and Julie's bedroom.

the problem

Alan and Julie Johnson's main bedroom is dated and devoid of character. The room is completely dominated by fitted wardrobes decorated with fussy panelling that take up almost two walls of the room. These culminate in a series of messy shelves stacked with plastic bags and old soft toys, that spill out over the floor. There is an old shag-pile carpet that has seen better days, the walls are covered in a nasty textured wallpaper and the padded bedhead needs replacing. The bed has a duvet cover but no bedspread, revealing the ugly bed base. The peach colour floral curtains are old and hanging off their rail; and the shade on the central pendant light is cheap-looking. The wall lights are broken and, to add insult to injury, there are no bedside tables and lamps for cosy reading in bed. Instead there is just a chair, which gets in the way of the door. The room needs a complete rethink.

the solution

This room is transformed by removing most of the fitted cupboards and rearranging the furniture. This makes the room appear much bigger and makes a feature of the bed. In a small bedroom, it is important to place the bed where it can have the maximum effect. The bed was next to the door, so you almost tripped over it as you entered.

The first task is to empty out the cupboards. Alan is a great hoarder and he is reluctant to throw out anything, so most of his clothes have to go into storage. The cupboards are reduced

from five to two and the fussy panelled doors are replaced with plain flush doors painted cream with sleek brushed steel handles. This frees up the wall furthest from the door, where the bed can now take pride of place.

There is no time to strip off the patterned wallpaper, so this is painted the same shade of cream as the two downstairs rooms. The neutral theme is continued with a new cream carpet and bed-linen. Two pale wood side tables and a chest of drawers, placed on the wall opposite the bed, are hired. The raffia lampshades on the two chrome bedside lamps add some interesting texture.

The highlight colours chosen for this room, a deep purple coupled with acid green and yellow, are not an obvious choice but are bold and unusual and work well in this sunny room. The bed's original padded bedhead is removed and a new one, upholstered in purple, is made and simply screwed to the wall behind. This is a simple trick that can be used to replace cumbersome bed-heads or where there is no bedhead at all.

In this bedroom, it is the cushions on the bed that immediately catch the eye and add a real touch of Hollywood glamour to the room. There are two expensive-looking, deep purple devoré cushions with greeny-yellow side panels and two smaller square cushions in the same greeny-yellow colour. The bed is given a final burst of colour with a purple waffle throw.

The chest of drawers facing the bed has a silver framed mirror above it to reflect light back into the room, and the green and maroon glass

left Drawers are hired to hold some of Alan's many clothes.

111

In a small bedroom, it is important to place the bed where it can have the maximum effect

112

vases holding chrysanthemums provide those all-important finishing touches that pull the look together. The room is completed with floaty muslin curtains in a sunny shade of acid yellow.

The finished room is completely unrecognisable. Whereas before it looked crowded and tired with no observable style, it is now transformed into a spacious bedroom with plenty of storage and a strong and unified sense of colour.

opposite The cushions and throw give the bed a touch of glamour.

113

left Coordinated bedside tables unify the room.

cost:
£780
including £90 for
furniture hire (per month)

brightening a dull bedroom

114

the problem

Sandra and Geoffrey Coleman's bedroom hasn't been redecorated since the couple moved into the house nine years ago and it is showing signs of neglect. The pink and purple zigzag wallpaper is dated, and the heavy purple curtains and duvet cover make the room dark and gloomy. The cup-boards don't match and the bedside tables are in a mess. There is a curious little shelving unit full of knick-knacks that would have looked happier in a child's bedroom in the 1950s. The only con-cession to the last ten years is a limed oak-effect laminate floor.

the solution

Give the room a lick of paint and a distinctive colour scheme to lighten and brighten it. Bedrooms are one of the few rooms where it can make sense to depart from the strictly neutral tones that work best in the rest of house. The Colemans' bedroom wallpaper is painted over with a pretty shade of pale green up to the picture rail. The walls above the picture rail, the ceiling and the paintwork are all given a coat of sparkling clean white paint. The cupboard is removed and put into storage and the heavy purple curtains and their mahogany pole are removed and replaced with simple white roman blinds.

The ugly yellow pine bed is disguised with new white bedlinen and four neatly stacked pink pillows. Pink is a colour that combines well with pale green to create a fresh, clean look. A deep pink cushion with a white, green and red chintz panel ties the whole look together.

above With pale bedding and walls, the room is transformed.

this bedroom is now light and airy rather than dull and dark

The bedside tables need taming. In this bedroom there is precious little space on either side of the bed. Two new matching tables are bought and placed lengthwise against the walls so that the door can open without obstruction. The clutter on the old tables is tidied up and everything that needs keeping is stored in little open wicker baskets. Rings and odd bits of jewellery can be popped into the two little wicker boxes with lids on the top of the table.

The dull white spotlight-style bedside lamps are replaced with attractive pale wood lamps with white shades. An unusual gold-painted small Lloyd Loom chair with the original green velvet fitted cushion matches the green colour scheme and brings a touch of classic style to the room. The chair is topped with a deep pink cushion, with the pink and green theme continued throughout the room in the choice of accessories. On the adjoining wall there are two of the chintz wallpaper pictures in white frames that feature throughout the house. This time the chintz is in shades of deep pink to match the colours used in the room.

This bedroom is now light and airy rather than dull and dark. With its pretty green and pink colour scheme and chintz pictures it is bound to be a big hit with female buyers. This is a point to bear in mind when doing up bedrooms. When it comes to buying family houses, it is usually the woman who has the final say, and an overly masculine main bedroom is likely to be a turn-off.

116 **opposite** A few carefully selected items placed on shelves, make the room more homely.

cost:
£267

injecting some style into a soulless bedroom

below Mismatched furniture and furnishings make this room look unloved.

the problem

Mark and Miriam Krepka's bedroom is painted a pretty shade of lilac, one of the very best colours for a bedroom. There is plenty of storage and an en suite bathroom, but the room lacks style. There is a double bed with an ugly bed base on show, an uninspired stripy duvet colour, and mismatched pillows. There are two bedside tables but these don't match either. The windows are obscured by the same old-fashioned flowery net curtains that feature throughout the house.

the solution

Move the bed, remove the net curtains, buy some smart new bedlinen, colour-coordinated cushions and new floaty curtains for a pretty feminine look. Double beds dominate most bedrooms so it is important to make a feature of them. The bed is moved from the wall nearest the door to the other side of the room where it can make a much bigger impact. The bed lacks a headboard, but as we saw in Alan and Julie Johnson's bedroom, a clever trick to save buying a new bed frame is to make a simple padded headboard and screw it directly to the wall behind the bed. Here the bedhead is covered with beige linen.

above The lilac colour scheme and pretty florals give the room a feminine look.

the bedroom is painted a pretty shade of lilac, one of the very best colours for a bedroom

Crisp new white bedlinen with a pattern of small tucks replaces the old duvet cover and pillows, and a matching white valance hides the bed base. The lilac theme is completed with two pretty toile de jouy-style covered pillows and two smaller square lilac cushions. Two simple, one-drawer bedside tables are hired for each side of the bed and topped with a plain black and white lamp.

The tuck detail on the bedlinen is picked up on the plain white curtains, which have a band of larger tucks near the top. A small pale wood chest of drawers on the wall opposite the bed has one of Mark and Miriam's wedding photographs in a Venetian-style mirror frame next to a crystal vase of pink roses. Three large lilac and blue flower prints in pale wooden frames add the final finishing touches.

This previously unloved room with its mismatched furniture now has a coherent style that puts the pretty colour of its lilac walls to good use.

above A wedding photo is a small, personal touch in a bedroom.

opposite The double bed dominates the room, but the fitted wardrobes will reassure a buyer that there's plenty of space.

cost:
£437
including £90 for furniture hire (per month)

Andrew says: Put stuff that you need day to day in stylish boxes and baskets, preferably with lids.

creating a bedroom with storage

above The arrangement of Gill's furniture doesn't make best use of the space.

the problem

The master bedroom in Gill Davis's flat is a mess. There is not enough storage space and the lighting is poor. There is a chest of drawers but no space for hanging Gill's designer wardrobe, and most of Gill's possessions are kept in an odd assortment of storage boxes stacked against the wall. Dry cleaning is hung on the door knob and a giant soft toy hippopotamus sits amid a jumble of Gill's make-up on top of the chest. There is no bedside lamp, which rules out reading in bed.

the solution

The room is given a fresh coat of paint, the storage is improved and the bed gets a splash of bright red. Gill's first task is to sift through the contents of the boxes on the bedroom floor and throw out anything that she doesn't need. The room is now given a coat of fresh white paint in place of the old magnolia. A simple fitted cupboard is made where Gill can hang at least some of her vast wardrobe. The cupboard's design is cheap but effective. A plain, white-painted MDF frame is fitted with two sliding panels that have white linen stretched over a frame, rather than solid doors. Fitted cupboards can appear to take up a lot of space but this

below Gill's clothes are stored in piled-up cardboard boxes, which might give a bad impression of the way Gill cares for her property.

Gill's first task was to sift through
the boxes on the floor and throw out
anything that she didn't need

design with its light fabric sliding panels works well in a small room.

The cupboard takes up the space previously occupied by the pine chest of drawers, which is now moved to the wall opposite the bed. What remains of the contents of Gill's boxes is placed in a neat row of eight identical white boxes.

The colour scheme is camel, which ties in with the colour chosen for the living room, and red, which picks up the accent colour in the kitchen. A plain new camel duvet cover is placed on the bed, along with two maroon cushions and two bright red cushions with a daisy pattern – another echo, this time of the motif in the kitchen. The dressing of the bed is completed with a bright red cable knit throw.

The red shaded bedside lamp provides a soft light for reading, and the black bowl filled with amber coloured crystals next to it gives a subtle sweet fragrance to the room.

The top of the chest of drawers is cleared of all its clutter of make-up and its giant stuffed toy hippopotamus. These are replaced with a pink orchid in a beige ceramic pot, a red and orange abstract print in a pale wood frame, a scented candle in a gold glass container, a cream hexagonal candle and a small perforated saucer with matching splashes of orange and red.

Gill's bedroom has now been transformed from a cluttered, unstructured mess, to a smart, grown-up, well-organised room with plenty of storage and a sense of style.

Andrew says: It's fine to have a laundry basket in your bedroom, but always keep it tidy or, ideally, have it hidden away.

left Matching storage boxes with lids form a cheap solution, and Gill can take them with her when she moves.

opposite Gill's bed is given prominence with bright cushions and a throw.

below A simple MDF cupboard is built in to appeal to buyers.

127

cost:
£250

chapter
nine

the
study

the study

A study can be a useful addition to a house, especially as an increasing number of people now work from home at least some of the time. However, if you only have two reception rooms, most buyers, especially families, expect to see them clearly defined as a separate living room and dining room, so converting a dining room into a study will not help you sell your house. Upstairs, too, a small room fitted out as a bedroom is more attractive to buyers than a house with fewer bedrooms and a study.

On the other hand, a small third reception room or a small box room make ideal studies, but decorating them offers a special challenge. Too often they become the private sanctuary of the men in the house – the twenty-first century equivalent of the garden shed – but this can make them appear cold and clinical.

Some families are very attached to their books, and although there is the old saying 'books do furnish a room', in reality too many books in the living room can make this important room look untidy. The study is the obvious place to store a family's book collection. If it doubles as the family library the addition of a couple of comfy chairs and a good reading light makes it a place that buyers can see is used by everyone in the family.

tips

Make it look comfortable. *Too often studies are dominated by a large, ugly computer, a printer and a trail of wires and cables. Think about moving a bulky computer out of the study while you are selling your house. On the other hand, a laptop, or a computer with a flat screen monitor, can give a study a chic and prosperous look. Make sure you turn the computer on with an attractive screen saver on display when viewers come round. Put in a comfortable chair and a reading light to give the impression that this is a quiet space where you come to read a book as well as do your paperwork.*

Andrew says: *Put yourself out.* Selling your house is all about inconvenience. If you don't put any effort in it could lose you thousands of pounds.

Invest in some shelves. A study can also double as a library, but don't use this as an excuse to hang on to books you will never read again. Arrange the books neatly on the shelves.

Think about storage. *A filing cabinet is fine in an office, but look for more attractive storage solutions for your home office. Storage boxes and files now come in a range of different materials, from expensive leather and medium-priced metal to cheap plastic and cardboard. Stack them tidily on some shelves neatly spaced to fit the size of the boxes or files you have chosen.*

Don't forget the accessories. Search out attractive accessories to bring order to your desk. A small filing tray, boxes for keeping all those odds and ends, such as paperclips and staples, and a pot for pens, give the impression of a well-ordered life.

Add a few feminine touches. *A picture or two and a houseplant may be all that is needed to take an overly masculine edge off a study.*

Make sure your shelves are flexible. Built-Built-in shelves are a neat solution in a study but if you are having them built, there is the temptation to design them around your storage needs. However, if you make sure the shelves are adjustable buyers can see that they will also suit their own, possibly very different, needs.

Tidy the bookshelves. *You might think that bookshelves bulging with books and CDs make you look like a cultured person. But the truth is buyers simply aren't interested in discovering your literary taste and even if they were, it probably wouldn't be the same as yours. Now is the time to be thinking about culling those never-to-be-read-again holiday paperbacks and five-year-old pop CDs. If you can't bring yourself to take them down to your local charity shop, put them in the attic or garage until you are ready to move. You can then make an attractive display of a pared-down selection of books and CDs. Arrange them by colour or by series. For example, a short run of the old-fashioned orange-spined Penguin books can add a splash of colour. A collection of travel books in the same series can be grouped together to good effect, and a small pile of old cloth-bound hardbacks with their mellow colours can look pretty.*

Put in a telephone socket. A study needs a telephone and an internet connection, so install an extra telephone socket or, better still, a separate line.

Andrew says: Think 'function' in a study area and ideally make sure it away from 'busy' parts of the home.

bringing a touch of comfort to a masculine study

below The Krepkas' study is dominated by computer equipment and books and is not a family space at all.

the problem

Mark Krepka's computer and dark wood computer table and furniture dominate the study in Mark and Miriam's house in Sandy in Bedfordshire. The room looks uncomfortable and unwelcoming.

this a room that *both* the owners of this house would use, not just the computer boffin

the solution

Create a reading area by removing Mark's bulky computer table with its old-fashioned monitor and keyboard to the garage whenever buyers come round and getting rid of some of the dark brown furniture. There are dark wood built-in shelves on both sides of the room and another tall freestanding bookshelf on the third wall. This is not a room anyone, except a real computer hobbyist like Mark, would want to spend any time in. In order to give the room a warmer, more welcoming feel, one set of built-in bookshelves

is removed. This is replaced with a cut-down version of the dark wood bookshelf, which is where Mark now neatly arranges his computer manuals.

Mark's computer is stacked under the shelf on the other side of the room. His smart flat screen monitor is placed on the shelf, which is wide enough to serve as a desk. The computer is switched on to show a colourful screen saver of swimming fishes.

The room is given a fresh coat of paint. A dark wood chair with a rush back is placed in the corner by the window, where it is the first thing you see on entering the room. The original green venetian blinds are retained, and a table lamp has been placed on top of the adjacent bookshelf. Buyers can now imagine themselves sitting and reading in here at night by the light of the lamp. A botanical print on the wall by the chair completes the message that this a room that *both* the owners of this house use, not just the computer boffin.

above Part of the room is given over to a reading chair and the books are less prominently displayed.

cost:
£141

chapter
ten

the
garden

the garden

A tidy front garden creates a good first impression and an outside eating area is always popular with buyers. Except in the city where outside space is a big selling point, gardens are rarely the deciding factor when it comes to selling your house. However, this doesn't mean you can ignore them, and just like any other aspect of your house, it is important to look at your garden through the eyes of your potential buyers.

Families with young children want houses with plenty of rough grass and tough shrubs where their growing offspring can kick a football around without doing too much damage. They won't be too impressed with elaborate planting schemes and island beds, and ponds – even those jumping with environmentally friendly frogs and newts – are a danger to young children. On the other hand, they will be pleased to find an eating-out area with a built-in barbecue for summer parties in the garden.

If you are selling an inner-city house or flat with a patio garden or roof terrace your likely buyer is probably a dedicated follower of the latest garden fashion. They won't want to encounter a litter-strewn patio with a few straggly plants. A quick makeover with gravel, a few evergreen plants in smart galvanised containers and some fashionable bamboos and grasses won't cost much, but will make a feature of your outdoor space, however small.

A low-maintenance garden with paving or gravel, and planted with mainly shrubs and trees, will appeal to the widest audience. Most buyers don't want to spend their life mowing lawns and tending to elaborate herbaceous borders. On the other hand, keen gardeners have a well-developed visual sense and won't have any problem planning how they will change a low-maintenance garden.

tips

Take care of basic maintenance. Make sure the front gate is freshly painted and the hinges oiled, and the front boundary wall is in good repair. In the back garden, check your fences are repaired, walls rebuilt and any trellis is firmly attached.

Tidy up. Sweep up the leaves, mow the grass, trim the hedges and weed the paths, and keep all trees and shrubs neatly pruned. You might let your garden die back naturally in winter, but buyers will not appreciate the wild winter look, so give the garden a good clear out before putting it on the market at this time of year.

Know the orientation of your garden. A south- or west-facing garden is a big plus, so always point it out. A north- or east-facing garden is less popular and you should keep quiet about it unless asked.

Andrew says: Make the most of what you have, whatever its size, and always create a seating area.

Think about removing trees that are too close to the house. If there is a large tree near the house, buyers will worry about subsidence. Take advice from a tree surgeon about whether it should be removed.

Invest in some evergreen plants and shrubs. These will remain green throughout the year and give your garden structure and year-round interest. These are particularly useful additions to your garden if you are selling in winter and most garden centres stock a good choice from September onwards.

Plant for privacy. Privacy is a big bonus. A garden that is not overlooked by its neighbours can be achieved almost anywhere with a combination of fencing and clever evergreen planting. But avoid the dense planting of conifer hedging such as the Leyland Cyprus which, unless kept frequently trimmed, is unattractive and sometimes leads to disputes with neighbours.

Put up a garden shed. A well-organised garden shed, which can be bought cheaply from do-it-yourself stores and garden centres provides buyers with somewhere to store their gardening equipment and the children's outdoor toys in winter. Rather than leave it with its original ugly orange wood stain colour, think about painting it a pretty shade of green or blue.

Clear the walls of invasive and rampant climbing plants. Non-clinging climbing plants well supported on trellis or wires, such as climbing roses and wisteria, will appeal to buyers, but climbers such as ivy can cause damage, so remove them and repair any problem areas.

Small gardens, patios, and roof terraces add value. In the city, a home with some sort of outdoor space always sells at a premium, so make the most of it. In small gardens, avoid using grass. It is difficult to maintain and there is rarely room to store a lawn mower. Gravel and paving are a better solution and don't cost much. Aim for a quite formal look with a restricted number of plants, such as fashionable box, bamboos and grasses. Invest in a few good quality terracotta pots and smart galvanised steel planters. Finally, make room for a table and chairs.

Pay attention to the lighting. Lighting extends the use of a garden, turning it into an outside room, and will appeal to buyers who see your garden first in the evening. Strings of outside fairy lights and spotlights which highlight certain plants and areas are easy to install. Candles placed in pretty lanterns add atmosphere.

Sell in the spring and summer. If you have a beautiful garden, it can be worth waiting until it is at its best – and for most gardens this means the spring and early summer – before putting it on the market.

137

converting a drab entrance into a smart outdoor eating area

the problem

To get to Alicia McDonnell's Manchester ground-floor, loft-style flat you pass through a dull courtyard, which is not creating the right first impression and is putting buyers off before they even reach the front door. Loft-style flats work better on upper floors where ceilings tend to be higher. In addition, the bedrooms in Alicia's flat are half underground, so she needs to compensate for this by showing the maximum potential of her outside space.

The addition of a small round outdoor table and two pretty slatted chairs complete the look

the solution

Define a pathway to the front door and create an outdoor eating area. Alicia's flat has its own dedicated outside area, which has been laid out with fashionable white granite chips and decking. At the moment Alicia is losing the opportunity to advertise this area as a place where you can sit and have a glass of wine at the end of a busy day.

The solution is simple: six small conifers are planted into smart stainless steel containers and

cost:
£300

139

above The first thing potential buyers will see as they approach Alicia's flat is a low-maintenance, but stylish and functional, outdoor space.

placed in two rows each side of the decking. The addition of a small round outdoor table and two pretty slatted chairs complete the look. It both defines a path to the front door but also shows the outdoor potential of the flat, compensating for the disadvantage of being on the ground floor.

Andrew says: Outside space at the front of your property creates an impression of what could be inside.

how the families fared

Coco and Tak Peppas

Coco and Tak Peppas's three-bedroom Victorian terrace house in Charlton, south-east London has been on the market for three months. They have had only six viewings and no offers. The couple are asking £240,000 but that is certainly more than the house is worth, because a similar house, in better condition, has recently sold for £10,000 less.

Coco and Tak and their three children, Si, Cole and Justy, need somewhere bigger to live. They have made an offer on a larger house just round the corner and they need to sell their house quickly for as much as possible otherwise the deal will fall through.

The house is taken off the market for four weeks and the team from *Selling Houses* gets to work. The house isn't selling because Coco and Tak's bohemian lifestyle doesn't appeal to the

kind of families who want to buy a house like this, and the best room in the house – the main bedroom – has been turned into a messy workshop.

Coco and Tak put their business on hold for a while and transform their old workshop into a chic and spacious double bedroom, with relaxing lilac paint and a modern steel framed bed. The hall and landing are given a coat of neutral paint for a fresh and airy feel. The second reception room, which had been used as a children's bedroom, is converted into a dining room. The house is now much more conventionally arranged to meet the expectations of the kind of professional families with young children who are buying these houses. The makeover costs the couple £1,085 which they hope to recoup when the house is sold.

The couple are now ready to put the house back on the market. The house was overpriced before, so they agree to drop the price by £5,000 to £235,000. In its former state the house was only worth £225,000. Coco and Tak need that extra £10,000 to clinch the deal on their new house and now, having spent just over £1,000, they are likely to get near the asking price. And it works. Just three weeks after the makeover, Coco and Tak accept an offer at the full asking price of £235,000 and are able to make the move to the larger house.

was worth:
£225,000
spent:
£1,085
sold for:
£235,000

chapter eleven

Dr Gary Wilbourne and Melanie Taylor

Dr Gary Wilbourne and Melanie Taylor's two-bedroom flat in Bedhampton near Portsmouth has been on the market for five months at £93,000. They have only had six viewings and one low offer. They want to move quickly because they have seen a three-bedroom semi-detached house in a nearby street that they like.

However, when the team from *Selling Houses* arrives, they find the couple resistant to change. They are very attached to the bright colour schemes that run through the flat and strongly object when their old, smelly carpet is replaced with a smart, modern coir carpet. Melanie dislikes it so much that Andrew Winter has to agree to replace the carpet if the flat doesn't sell in four weeks.

The couple's huge Rottweiler is a big drawback. This kind of dog can be very intimidating, and Gary and Melanie are probably not aware that a doggy smell pervades the whole flat; the only way to get rid of it is to replace the carpets throughout.

Nor is Gary's collection of guns and knives, which is displayed on the hall walls and the second bedroom, giving out a very friendly message. Once the carpets are ripped up and the couple's surplus clutter and Gary's armoury have gone into storage, the flat is ready for its makeover. The living room is well decorated, but the furniture is rearranged to give more clearly defined seating and dining areas. The kitchen gets a new colour scheme. The room is light so it can take a strong colour. The walls are painted Victorian red, the dated pine units are painted off-white, and a new vinyl floor is laid. The shocking pink shower room is painted white, which makes it seem much bigger, and the cluttered box room is converted back into a second bedroom. The gaudy master bedroom is painted a restful shade of blue and floaty muslin curtains filter the light.

The makeover costs Gary and Melanie £986, of which £650 is spent on the new coir carpet. But will it get them the offer they need? Melanie has to eat her words when one potential buyer mentions just how nice the carpet is. Then things move very fast. The first person to view puts in an offer. So after five months languishing on the market, the flat is finally sold for the full asking price on the day it goes back on sale. Not bad.

unsold for:
five months
spent:
£986
good offer in:
one day

Ann Stolworthy

142

Ann Stolworthy and her two teenage daughters, Ali and Katie, have been trying to sell their seventeenth-century cottage in the Staffordshire village of Alton for six months at an asking price of £160,000, but so far no one has made an offer. They would like to move to a newly built four-bedroom house on a nearby development.

Ann's cottage isn't selling because it has an unusual layout. There is a lot of clutter, which makes the rooms seem small, the colour schemes are dark and gloomy and the spaces aren't clearly defined. When the *Selling Houses* team arrive they diagnose the problems straight away and set to work giving the cottage a bright, new white colour scheme with splashes of bold red. This makes the rooms seem much larger and emphasises the beautiful old oak beams, while retaining the cottagey feel so loved by people who are attracted to this sort of property and the country life.

There are three separate reception rooms on the ground floor. The first room is nothing more than a walk-through even though it has a lovely stone inglenook fireplace. This room is painted white and turned into a dining room. The second room, previously a teenage bedroom complete with an enormous sunbed, becomes a cosy television room. The third reception room is a beautiful airy room, open to the rafters with French windows leading to the garden. Here the terracotta rag-rolled walls and the leafy mural on the ceiling are given a coat of white paint. Upstairs, the main bedroom is given a good spring clean and the pretty cast-iron fireplace is revealed to become the main feature of the room. The disastrous bathroom with its grimy cracked tiles and mould is transformed with a new white bathroom suite.

The cottage is now ready to receive its first viewers. Before the makeover Andrew Winter estimates that Ann would have had to drop her asking price from £160,000 to £145,000. The work to her cottage has cost her around £1,200 and Andrew is now convinced that she will get her asking price of £160,000. So for a small outlay, she should make a profit of nearly £14,000.

But it doesn't go quite as smoothly as Ann hopes. The third couple to view the cottage put in a low offer, which annoys Ann because she doesn't think they are serious. However, a week later, they come back and offer the full asking price, which means that Ann and her daughters can now make the move to the new house they have set their hearts on.

was worth:
£145,000
spent:
£1,200
sold for:
£160,000

Sean and Alison Blake

Sean and Alison Blake's three-bedroom semi-detached, former council house in the pretty Essex village of Latchington has been on the market for nine months for £125,000. The couple want to move closer to Sean's job in Milton Keynes and they need to get a good price for the house.

The home is spacious and should appeal to young families, but when the *Selling Houses* team arrive they are confronted with the first problem – the house has no proper front door. And there are other reasons why the house isn't appealing to families. The kitchen is small and the upstairs bathroom lacks a toilet. Plus the main bedroom is painted a garish shade of pink, which won't appeal to everyone.

Using a good deal of ingenuity, the team set to work solving these defects. The entrance hall is revamped and the kitchen is extended into the lean-to conservatory. The bathroom upstairs gets a new bathroom suite and the much-needed toilet. The main bedroom is painted a neutral shade and, finally, the greenhouse in the garden is dismantled to reveal a lovely view over open fields, which will be a big selling point.

The work including labour costs £1,800. This is a high price to pay but Andrew Winter is convinced that without spending this money, Sean and Alison would have to cut the asking price by £10,000 to £115,000. Now they can confidently ask for £125,000, which they need if they are to buy the sort of house they would like in Milton Keynes.

The house has been on the market for nine months with no interest, but now just hours after the house goes back on sale, Alison and Sean get an offer. Even better, later on the same day, they get an even higher offer, which they are happy to accept.

was worth:
£115,000
spent:
£1,800
sold in one day for:
£125,500

Gay and Keith Keaveny

In spite of dropping the asking price on their Croydon house by £30,000 to £300,000, Gay and Keith Keaveny still haven't found a buyer. The house has been on the market for seven months. The couple and their two teenage sons are planning a complete change of lifestyle with a move to a farmhouse in the south of France – which might fall through if they can't sell quickly.

On the face of it this good-looking tile hung 1980s house, with its double garage and imposing front drive, should appeal to professional families who come to live in Croydon for its excellent schools and fast train service to London.

The reason why this house isn't selling is clear once the team from *Selling Houses* steps inside. The house has had very little done to it since the mid-1980s and the décor is tired. For this kind of price, buyers expect to find a much more up-to-date look.

The downstairs rooms are all linked, but the hall is cluttered and the living room and dining room are decorated in clashing styles. Upstairs the family bathroom has a gloomy grey suite, and the fourth bedroom is being used as a study.

The remedy is simple. The team sweeps up the family's surplus clutter and puts it into storage along with the heavy dining room furniture. In the living room, the 1980s vinyl wallpaper cannot be painted over, so Gay invites her netball team round and they set to work with the steam stripper. A unified contemporary look is created with neutral paint and a wood laminate floor. In the dining room, a pale modern dining table and chairs are hired. Upstairs the bathroom gets new white tiles and the fourth bedroom is converted back into a bedroom.

The transformation has cost the Keavenys £1,000, but is it going to do the trick? It seems the *Selling Houses* team has worked its magic once again. After just four viewings, the Keavenys get the offer they have been waiting seven months for.

unsold for:
seven months

spent:
£910

sold for:
£300,000

Alicia McDonnell

Alicia McDonnell bought her ground-floor warehouse-style flat in central Manchester as an investment. She was renting it out, but now it is empty and she has been trying to sell it for over a year, because she would like to move to a house in the leafy Manchester suburb of Didsbury. She is asking £126,000 for the flat, but there is a lot of competition from new loft-style developments in the area, and she may be asking too much money.

According to Andrew Winter, she doesn't stand a chance of getting this price unless she tackles some of the flat's fundamental problems. At the moment, the flat is dull and dreary. It is furnished with junkshop finds and won't appeal to the sort of young professionals who are looking for a cool inner-city pad.

The solution is to put most of the Alicia's furniture into storage and hire entirely new furniture to give the flat a stylish new look. In the large open-plan living room the bleak concrete ceiling is painted a neutral colour, and two distinct areas are defined, one for sitting and one for dining. Smart new modern furniture is installed. The kitchen is cheered up with new lighting and a coat of paint.

The two semi-basement bedrooms look too subterranean, so the bare brick is painted a neutral colour, brightly coloured panels are hung on the walls, and the windows get fashionable blinds.

The bathroom is well fitted out, but benefits from the addition of a new shower curtain. Being on the ground floor, Alicia has the advantage of some outside space, which she is failing to exploit. The addition of a row of conifers and an outside table and chairs help define the entrance to the flat and provide a seating area. Outside space is at a premium in the inner city. Before, buyers had no idea that Alicia's flat had such an amenity.

Alicia's makeover has cost £1,700 including the hire of the furniture. Alicia shows a real talent for selling and the flat now hits all the right buttons with the young professionals who come to view it. But will she get the price she wants? After a year on the market, Alicia finally gets her first offer, but with the competition so hot in this fast-expanding inner-city location, it is £3,000 short of her asking price. It isn't quite what Alicia had hoped for but she has made a profit and more importantly she can now buy the home she wants in the suburbs.

unsold for:
over a year
spent:
£1,700
sold for:
£123,000

Alan and Julie Johnson

Alan and Julie Johnson's four-bedroom 1930s family house on one of the best roads in Hornchurch in Essex is proving surprisingly hard to sell. It has been on the market for four months and they have had only eight viewings and no offers. This is delaying the family's plan to move to Lincolnshire where Julie's parents live.

This is potentially a lovely, spacious family house, but the *Selling Houses* team can see immediately that the tired décor and the arrangement of the rooms is putting off the buyers. There is still a long way to go before the house will find someone prepared to pay the asking price of £320,000 which is top whack for the area.

The four rooms that need attention are the kitchen, the two reception rooms and the main bedroom. These are key rooms that need to be in tip-top condition with that sought-after designer look if Alan and Julie are to leave Hornchurch with a pocketful of cash.

The couple have owned the house for thirty years and some of the rooms have hardly changed over the years. Modern furniture is hired to give the front reception room a clean, contemporary look. The long back room, which had been used as a sitting room, now becomes the dining room, with a reading area at the end. The bare brick in the country-style kitchen is painted a neutral colour and, with the big American-style fridge put into storage, there is now room for a small family eating area.

Upstairs, the main bedroom gets a glamorous makeover. The cupboards are reduced in number, new furniture is hired and the room gets a clever maroon and acid green colour scheme.

Alan and Julie have spent £2,700, including £270 for a month's furniture rental. Like many vendors, the Johnsons found it difficult to spend money on a house they were leaving behind. But the truth is, without tackling the property's key problems, they could never hope to get the top price.

unsold for:
four months

spent:
£2,700

had an offer for:
£310,000

Gill Davis

Beauty consultant Gill Davis's two-bedroom attic flat in Surbiton in Surrey has been on the market with an asking price of £185,000 for a year, and although thirty to forty people have been to see it, she has only had one offer of £180,000, which she turned down.

So what is going on? Surbiton is a popular location, with a village atmosphere and an excellent train service to London. Gill's flat is in a listed converted Victorian house in the best square in the town, where flats normally sell very quickly.

But Gill's flat is failing to impress the buyers and when the *Selling Houses* team arrives they are quick to explain why. Gill's flat has a lovely spacious reception area, a good-sized double bedroom, a smaller second bedroom and a kitchen and a bathroom. But the décor won't appeal to the young professional buyers who are her target market. Nor will they be happy to pay £185,000 for a flat with no cooker and no eating area.

Gill's living room furniture goes into storage, and smart new furniture is hired. A new dining table and chairs are installed in the living room, to create a dining area. In the bedroom, new matching storage boxes take care of Gill's clutter which is scattered around the flat or stored in old cardboard boxes. The room has no hanging space so a cupboard with sliding doors is built. The kitchen gets a cooker and the look is streamlined with new cabinet doors and brushed steel handles.

The second bedroom is cleared of all its rubbish, and the hall door gets a coat of fresh blue paint.

The makeover has cost Gill around £2,000 including hiring the furniture for a month. The flat now has the kind of contemporary style that will appeal to young professionals. The makeover has been so successful that Andrew Winter advises Gill to increase the asking price to £199,000 in order to attract a slightly wealthier class of house hunter. This is a clever trick. By positioning her flat in a more expensive price bracket, people who haven't seen it before and who have more money to spend will come to view it. Without this price hike Andrew Winter thinks she might only get another low offer. The advice is sound. Someone who saw the flat in its previous incarnation, and who rejected it without making an offer, now offers to buy it for £185,000, Gill's original asking price.

unsold for:
one year
spent:
£2,000
had an offer for:
£185,000

how to sell your house

Buying and selling houses is a nerve-wracking business and the way the law works in England and Wales doesn't help. There can be months of nail-biting negotiations before you finally know if the buyer you have lined up for your house is going to come through with the money. And when you are buying a house there can be similar delays while the vendor decides if he wants to go through with the sale.

The law in Scotland is rather different, and although the deal is struck at an earlier stage and there is much less uncertainty, the system is not without its problems. For example, it can be difficult to synchronise buying and selling, which often involves some sort of bridging loan that is not common in the rest of the UK.

prepare your own seller's pack

The government has promised to reform the way we buy and sell houses in England and Wales. It intends introducing 'seller's packs' from 2005. These are designed to speed up the selling process by requiring the seller to prepare a pack of information for the buyer before the house goes on sale. This would include the searches, a basic survey and, for a leasehold property, a copy of the lease. The aim is to cut down the time between the acceptance of an offer and exchange of contracts in order to reduce the opportunities for gazumping and 'gazundering'.

However, if you want to speed up your own sale before the introduction of seller's packs, there is nothing to stop you preparing your own pack of information now. What's the point of spending weeks preparing your house and clearing away the clutter, if you can't make a quick sale because you haven't got the paperwork sorted.

Ask your solicitor or licensed conveyancer to conduct the searches before you put the house on the market. You may meet resistance to this proposal, but be firm, you are not asking for anything illegal. The searches are valid for three months, but if you have followed all the advice in this book, you will have sold your house by then.

Ask a surveyor to conduct a survey of your house. If you had one done when you bought the house, you can ask the same surveyor to update it for you, which should save you some money. You will have to pay for the survey, but you can make it a condition of any sale that some or all of the cost is borne by the eventual buyer. Some buyers feel they can't trust a report commissioned by the seller. To get round this, make sure the surveyor is happy to assign the report to the eventual buyers, so that if anything goes wrong the buyers have the right to sue the surveyor.

estate agents

Estate agents vary in the amount of commission they charge. There may be many reasons why you might not want to go with the agent charging the cheapest commission. Not many people

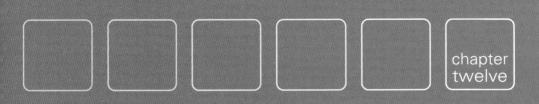

agent. However, estate agents don't charge for valuations. Get at least four firms to value your house, and just be vague about your plans to sell. It is a good idea to make yourself a smart 'for sale' board. Advertise your house in the local paper using a good quality exterior shot of the house, and investigate advertising on the Internet. Compile your own property details, using examples gathered from local estate agents. Good quality photographs can act as a useful memory aid for buyers when they get home and weigh up the various houses they have seen. Private buyers, unlike estate agents, are not bound by the Property Misdescriptions Act, but check it anyway to make sure you aren't making exaggerated claims for your house.

left First 151
impressions
count, so give
your front door a
fresh coat of
paint.

realise that the amount of commission is negotiable. For example, you might be able to negotiate an agent who normally charges 2.25 per cent down to 1.75 or 2 per cent. However, to avoid arguments later, it is important to have this in writing and inserted in your contract. Also, estate agents try and tie you to an exclusive contract for twelve weeks or three months. An estate agent who can't sell your house in four weeks is not worth his salt, so only agree to sign up for four weeks, after which you will be free to take your business elsewhere.

It is perfectly legal to dispense with the services of an estate agent if you are determined to save money. Fixing the right selling price is the main problem of going it alone without an estate

how to sell your house on the day

So your house is ready. It is spick and span and looks like a show house. You are waiting expectantly, and probably rather nervously, for that knock on the door from your first potential buyers. Experienced estate agents such as Andrew Winter have all sorts of little psycholog-

Andrew says: If you can't sell your house and you can't be bothered to improve the presentation, **drop the price**. It will work.

above Keep pets out of the way when viewers come round.

ical tricks up their sleeves designed to turn viewers into buyers. However, you won't necessarily always have an estate agent on hand to show people around, so it is worth picking up a few tips from those in the know.

Buyers are reputed to make up their minds about a house within the first eleven seconds. This means the front garden, the front door and the hall must make a good first impression. Hide any pets away. No one wants to be greeted by your dog's muddy paws on their clean coat, or sit on a sofa covered in cats' hairs.

Don't greet the buyer with too much visual information at once. For example, if there is an attractive view from the hall into, say, the kitchen, then show it, but close all the other doors off the hall, so that these rooms come as a surprise.

Carefully guide the viewer round the house. Make sure they see the house in the order you decide, but give the buyer the impression that they are in control by letting them enter each room first with you following. If you decide to show the best rooms first, make sure they also see them again before they leave.

On the first viewing be businesslike, rather than overly friendly. Buyers are usually busy people and they may have booked to see several houses that day. The last thing they want to hear is your life story.

It is useful to have compiled a fact file about your house. For example, if the property is leasehold, the lease and details of the service charge should be available. Compile a list of the utility companies and how much the bills come to. Make sure you have the service manuals and servicing record for the boiler and any appliances you are selling with the house. Also, it is worth drawing up a list of which fixtures and fittings are included in the price and which you want to take with you or sell separately. A list of local schools and doctors' surgeries should also be included.

However, don't bombard your viewers with this information on their first visit. It is too much information to take in, and if they aren't remotely interested in buying your house, it is simply a waste of everyone's time. Remember that at this preliminary stage, they are simply viewing your house. However, if they are interested, they may ask more questions, in which case the information will be efficiently at hand.

If they come back for a second visit, it shows they are keen. Now, it pays to be more friendly. Offer your buyers a coffee and let them know you have a file of information about the house and the neighbourhood, which you are happy to let them consult. But don't be too keen or pushy, and if there are other buyers who seem interested, it is worth dropping this casually into the conversation.

Always accentuate the positive and don't draw attention to negative factors. For example, a room overlooking the garden but with a busy road at the bottom should elicit a comment such as: 'This room is lovely and airy and has a wonderful view of the garden,' and not, 'We have got used to the noise of the traffic.'

Buyers invariably ask why you are moving. Have your answer ready and think of one – it doesn't need to be a lie – that doesn't cast your present house in a bad light. So: 'We need somewhere larger' is not a good answer because it implies that your current house is small, but 'We both work from home and need a home with space for a workshop and an office,' doesn't imply that your current house is too small, just that it no longer suits your very particular needs.

In spite of Andrew Winter's extensive coaching in the art of showing a house to its best advantage, most of our house sellers made one or two basic errors. Alison Blake is too friendly and chatty with her viewers and makes the mistake of giving too much information. In her enthusiasm for the wildlife in her garden, she mentions seeing snakes, which is likely to put off most buyers, especially those with children. She then refers to one of the rooms as the smallest. There is no need to refer to anything negative such as this. Buyers can work it out for themselves.

Gay Keaveny was caught making a dash to put down the toilet seat. As Andrew Winter says, this breaks two golden rules. The inside of a toilet is not the strongest feature of any house, so leave all toilet seats and covers down. And in her anxiety to put the toilet seat down, she barged into the room before her buyer. Ann Stolworthy promises to keep the dog out of the house while viewings are going on but forgets, and the dog is found sleeping on one of the upstairs beds.

Coco Peppas make the same mistake with her cat, which is spotted by a viewer who is allergic to cat fur. Andrew discusses the order in which Coco should show the house, starting with the stunning lilac bedroom. On the first viewing Coco is indecisive and lets the buyer into the sitting room first. When another buyer asks about the laminate flooring in the dining room she becomes flustered and talks about it being laid on top of something she dreads to think about, unnecessarily alerting her buyer to a potential problem.

tips

- First impressions count, so pay particular attention to front gardens, porches and halls.
- *Make sure windows are sparkling clean and curtains are evenly and neatly drawn.*
- Air the house by opening the windows for a blast of fresh air a couple of hours before any viewings.
- *If it is a dull day, light the table lamps to give a restful, cosy atmosphere.*
- Light scented candles if you are worried about unwanted pet or cooking smells.
- *Avoid viewings at meal times.*
- Put pets in the garden.
- *Fresh flowers make a good impression.*
- Don't give the buyer too much visual information all at once. Leave most doors closed.
- *Give buyers the impression of control by letting them enter each room first.*
- Be businesslike on the first visit.
- *Be more friendly on the second visit.*
- Decide in what order you are going to show the house. Show the best rooms first and/or last.
- *Emphasise the positive and don't draw attention to bad points.*
- Think of positive answers to questions that you might be asked, such as 'Why are you moving?'

below Display fresh flowers, but throw them out at the first sign of wilt.

153

source book

professional services

**The Records Department
The Law Society**
Ipsley Court
Berrington Close
Redditch B98 0TD
0870 6066575
www.solicitors-online.com

**The Royal Institute of
British Architects**
66 Portland Place
London W1B 1AD
020 7580 5533
www.architecture.com

**The Royal Institution of
Chartered Surveyors**
Surveyor Court
Westwood Way
Coventry CV4 8JE
0870 3331600
www.rics.org

**Council of Licensed
Conveyancers**
16 Glebe Road
Chelmsford
Essex CM1 1QG
01245 349599
www.theclc.gov.uk

The Building Centre
26 Store Street
London WC1E 7BT
020 7692 4000
www.buildingcentre.co.uk

**The Federation of Master
Builders**
Gordon Fisher House
14–15 Great James Street
London WC1N 3DP
020 7242 2200
www.fmb.org.uk

self storage

**The Big Yellow Storage
Company**
0800 783 4949
www.thebigyellow.co.uk

Spaces Personal Storage
0800 622244
www.spaces.uk.com

furniture hire

Roomservice Group
28 Barwell Business Park
Leatherhead Road
Chessington
Surrey KT9 2NY
020 8397 9344
www.roomservicegroup.com

**The Contract Furniture
Specialists**
9 Warple Mews
Warple Way
Acton
London W3 0RF
020 8743 5535
www.tcfslondon.com

**McGlashan's Property
Services**
43 Marylebone Lane
London W1U 2NS
0207 486 6711
www.mcglashans.co.uk

paint

Dulux
ICI Paints
Wexham Road
Slough SL2 5DS
01753 550555
www.dulux.co.uk

Fired Earth
Twyford Mill
Oxford Road
Adderbury
Banbury
Oxfordshire OX17 3HP
01295 814315
www.firedearth.co.uk

Crown
PO Box 37
Crown House
Hollins Road
Darwen Road
Lancashire BB3 0BG
01254 704951
www.crownpaint.co.uk

Sanderson Spectrum
Sanderson House
Oxford Road
Denham
Buckinghamshire UB9 4DX
01895 830044
www.sanderson-online.co.uk

accessories

B & Q
1 Hampshire Corporate Park
Chandlers Ford
Eastleigh
Hampshire SO53 3YX
02380 256256
www.diy.com

BoConcept
Parkway House
28 Avenue Road
Bournemouth BH2 56L
0845 6050565
www.boconcept.co.uk

Bodum (UK) Ltd
Grange Park 1
Cheaney Drive
Grange Park South
Northampton NN4 5FB
01604 826888
www.bodum.com

Brabantia (UK) Ltd
Blackfriars Road
Nailsea
Bristol BS48 4SB
01275 810600
www.brabantia.com

Habitat
42-46 Princelet Street
London EC1 5LP
09845 6010740
www.habitat.net

IKEA
Glasgow: 0141 885 2281
Edinburgh: 0131 448 0500
Warrington: 01925 655 889
Gateshead: 0191 461 0202
Leeds: 01924 423 296
Nottingham: 0115 938 6888
Bristol: 0117 927 6001
Wednesbury: 0121 526 5232
Thurrock: 01708 860 868
Croydon: 020 8208 5601
Brent Park: 020 8208 5600
www.ikea.co.uk

Laura Ashley
Customer Service
PO Box 19
Newtown
Powys SY16 1DZ
0870 5622 116
www.lauraashley.com

window treatments

Swish
Newell Window Fashions
Litchfield Industrial Estate
Tamworth
Staffordshire BT9 7TW
01827 64242

electrical appliances

Stoves
Stoney Lane
Prescot
Merseyside L35 2XW
0151 432 7838
www.stoves.co.uk

Hotpoint
Consumer Service Division
Morley Way
Peterborough
Cambridgeshire PE2 9JB
08701 506070
www.hotpoint.co.uk

lighting

QVS
168 Brighton Road
Coulsden
Surrey CR5 2NE
020 8763 1500
www.qvselectricalwholesale.co.uk

carpets

Riverdale Flooring
Unit 2
Hillsborough Trading Estate
Hillsborough
Sheffield
S6 1PG
0114 2333033

155

pricing the makeover

kitchens

	specification	prices from
Worksurfaces:		
Plain white laminated chipboard	3 metres	£20.00
Granite patterned laminated chipboard	3 metres	£30.00
Kitchen doors:		
Sheet of 9mm MDF	0.6 x 1.3 metres	£6.00
Replacement doors	0.6 metres wide	£27.00
Kitchen cabinets:		
Standard base unit (without doors)	0.6 metres wide	£23.00
Standard wall unit (without doors)	0.6 metres wide	£18.00
Handles:		
Pair of long brushed steel handles		£8.00
Pair of short brushed steel handles		£4.00
Taps:		
Basic chrome kitchen mixer taps		£20.00
Designer chrome kitchen mixer taps		£35.00
Cooking appliances:		
Built-in hob with four burners		£99.00
Built-in fan oven		£200.00

bathrooms

		prices from
Bathroom suite:		
White bath		£130.00
Basin, pedestal		£66.00
Toilet, cistern, lever, seat		£140.00
Showers:		
Shower attachment		£30.00
Electric shower		£65.00
Mixer shower		£100.00
Shower pump (not for use with combination boilers or pressurised systems)		£120.00
Accessories:		
White plastic lavatory seat		£10.00
Shower curtain		£10.00
Cleaning:		
Mould remover		£5.00
Grout cleaner		£6.00
Tile cleaner		£7.00

flooring

		prices from
Wood laminate	per square metre	£8.00
Vinyl	per square metre	£6.00
Vinyl tiles	per square metre	£4.00

item	specification	prices from
Quarry tile	per square metre	£16.00
Ceramic tile	per square metre	£9.00
Slate	per square metre	£7.75
Wool-style coir	per square metre	£8.00
Coir	per square metre	£12.00
Sisal	per square metre	£12.00
Sea grass	per square metre	£18.00
Plain twist pile	per square metre	£6.00

tiles

Plain white tiles	per square metre	£4.00

paint

Brilliant white emulsion	10 litres*	£10.00
Magnolia/cream/neutral emulsions	2.5 litres**	£12.00
Pale coloured emulsions	2.5 litres**	£12.00
White gloss or satinwood	2.5 litres ***	£10.00
Floor paint	2.5 litres****	£20.00

lighting

In the house:

Pack of five halogen downlighters	£23.00
One halogen downlighter	£8.00
Ceramic wall lights	£15.00
Cream ceramic table lamp	£12.00
Cream/beige suede-effect lamp shade	£10.00

In the garden:

Solar powered uplighter (limited winter light)	£15.00
Pack of four glass globe low-voltage lights	£30.00
Halogen deck light	£19.50

storage

25 square feet of storage	£47–£75 per 4-week period

furniture hire

Sofa	from £20 a week
Rug	from £10 a week
Lamp	from £5 a week
Double bed	from £10 a week
Dining table and four chairs	from £35 a week

* covers 140 square metres, enough to paint two medium-sized rooms
** covers 30 square metres, enough to paint half a medium-sized room
*** covers 25 square metres, enough to paint both sides of five doors
**** covers 40 square metres, enough to paint one large room

index

acknowledgements

The author would like to thank the production team at Ricochet South, and in particular Liz Dyson and the designers Lizzie Chambers and Emma McKelvie for their friendly and efficient cooperation during the writing of this book. Thanks are also due to the families who allowed me to the visit their homes, especially Alan and Julie Johnson in Hornchurch and Mark and Miriam Krepka in Sandy who took so much pleasure in the project.

picture credits

Ricochet South: 14, 15, 16, 17, 34 (both), 35 (right), 42 (both), 44, 46, 48, 52 (top), 54 (top), 62, 64, 68, 70, 76, 78, 82, 86, 88, 89, 92, 98, 108, 110 (both), 114, 118, 120, 124, 125, 132 (both), 146, 147, 148, 149.

Paul Bricknell: 38/9, 49, 50, 51 (both), 52 (bottom), 53, 54 (bottom), 55, 56/7, 65, 66, 67, 69, 71, 72/3, 83, 84/5, 87, 90, 90/1, 93 (both), 102/3, 111, 112/3, 113, 115, 116/7, 121, 122, 123, 126, 127 (both), 128/9, 133.

Tim Anderson: 6, 7 (left and bottom right), 8, 9, 11, 12, 35 (left), 37, 43 (both), 47, 60, 60/1, 63, 99, 109, 140, 141, 143, 144.

Bill Stephenson: 7 (top right), 10, 13, 45, 77, 79, 80, 80/1, 101, 119, 134/5, 138/9, 142, 145,

EWA: 20 (Dominic Whiting), 27 (Tommy Candler), 29 (Rodney Hyett), 151 (Adam Papadatos), 152 (Di Lewis).

Robert Harding: 18 (Nigel Francis), 19 (Roy Rainford), 25 (Polly Wreford /Inspirations), 28 (Simon Whitmore/Inspirations), 30/1(Stewart Grant/ Inspirations), 94/5 (Jon Bouchier/Inspirations), 153 (Nick Pope/Inspirations).

Arcaid: 22 (Nicholas Kane), 23 (Richard Bryant), 24 (Premium), 26 (Premium).

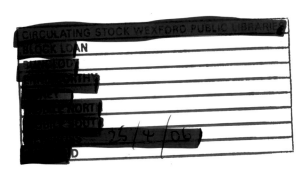